STERLING BIOGRAPHIES

THOMAS JEFFERSON

Architect of Freedom

Rita Thievon Mullin

To my sons, Michael and Matthew, whose curiosity,
creativity, and humor inspire me daily

Acknowledgments

Special thanks to Michael and Matthew Mullin and Laura Hadley, whose comments on each
chapter strengthened the text immeasurably. Thanks to my editors, Heather Quinlan and Rick
Ball, who offered sure, steady hands in helping shape the book. Finally, thanks to the librarians at
the Fairfax Regional Library of the Fairfax Public Library System for their assistance in locating
volumes and to Anna Berkes, reference librarian at the Jefferson Library in Charlottesville,
Virginia, for her guidance on valuable primary sources at the beginning of my journey.

Library of Congress Cataloging-in-Publication Data

Mullin, Rita T.
  Thomas Jefferson : architect of freedom / Rita Mullin.
      p. cm. -- (Sterling biographies)
  Includes bibliographical references and index.
  ISBN-13: 978-1-4027-3397-0
  ISBN-10: 1-4027-3397-6
  1. Jefferson, Thomas, 1743-1826--Juvenile literature. 2. Presidents--United States--Biography--
Juvenile literature. I. Title.

E332.79.M85 2007
973.4'6092--dc22
[B]
                                                                            2006027365

10 9 8 7 6 5 4 3 2

Published by Sterling Publishing Co., Inc.
387 Park Avenue South, New York, NY 10016
© 2007 by Rita Thievon Mullin
Distributed in Canada by Sterling Publishing
c/o Canadian Manda Group, 165 Dufferin Street
Toronto, Ontario, Canada M6K 3H6
Distributed in the United Kingdom by GMC Distribution Services Castle Place,
166 High Street, Lewes, East Sussex, England BN7 1XU
Distributed in Australia by Capricorn Link (Australia) Pty. Ltd.
P.O. Box 704, Windsor, NSW 2756, Australia

Printed in China
All rights reserved

Sterling ISBN-13: 978-1-4027-3397-0 (paperback)
      ISBN-10: 1-4027-3397-6

Sterling ISBN-13: 978-1-4027-4750-2 (hardcover)
      ISBN-10: 1-4027-4750-0

Designed by Joe Borzetta
Image research by Susan Schader

For information about custom editions, special sales, premium
and corporate purchases, please contact Sterling Special Sales
Department at 800-805-5489 or specialsales@sterlingpub.com.

Contents

Events in the Life of Thomas Jefferson

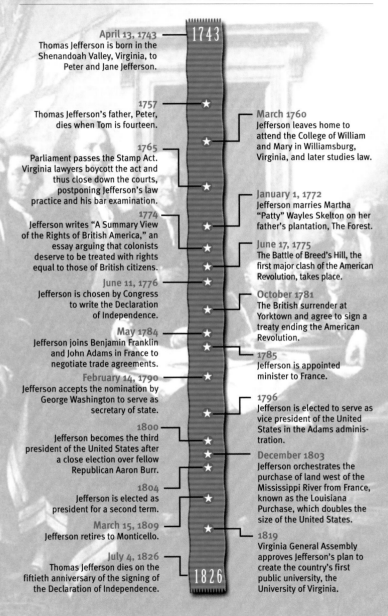

1743

April 13, 1743
Thomas Jefferson is born in the Shenandoah Valley, Virginia, to Peter and Jane Jefferson.

1757
Thomas Jefferson's father, Peter, dies when Tom is fourteen.

March 1760
Jefferson leaves home to attend the College of William and Mary in Williamsburg, Virginia, and later studies law.

1765
Parliament passes the Stamp Act. Virginia lawyers boycott the act and thus close down the courts, postponing Jefferson's law practice and his bar examination.

January 1, 1772
Jefferson marries Martha "Patty" Wayles Skelton on her father's plantation, The Forest.

1774
Jefferson writes "A Summary View of the Rights of British America," an essay arguing that colonists deserve to be treated with rights equal to those of British citizens.

June 17, 1775
The Battle of Breed's Hill, the first major clash of the American Revolution, takes place.

June 11, 1776
Jefferson is chosen by Congress to write the Declaration of Independence.

October 1781
The British surrender at Yorktown and agree to sign a treaty ending the American Revolution.

May 1784
Jefferson joins Benjamin Franklin and John Adams in France to negotiate trade agreements.

1785
Jefferson is appointed minister to France.

February 14, 1790
Jefferson accepts the nomination by George Washington to serve as secretary of state.

1796
Jefferson is elected to serve as vice president of the United States in the Adams administration.

1800
Jefferson becomes the third president of the United States after a close election over fellow Republican Aaron Burr.

December 1803
Jefferson orchestrates the purchase of land west of the Mississippi River from France, known as the Louisiana Purchase, which doubles the size of the United States.

1804
Jefferson is elected as president for a second term.

March 15, 1809
Jefferson retires to Monticello.

1819
Virginia General Assembly approves Jefferson's plan to create the country's first public university, the University of Virginia.

July 4, 1826
Thomas Jefferson dies on the fiftieth anniversary of the signing of the Declaration of Independence.

1826

An American Life

We hold these truths to be self-evident, that all men are created equal, that they are endowed by their Creator with certain unalienable Rights, that among these are Life, Liberty, and the pursuit of Happiness.

Few words have caused more change in the world than these. Thomas Jefferson wrote them in the Declaration of Independence in 1776. Jefferson was a great thinker whose ideas helped shape America in its early years and who continues to influence the ideals of this country today.

It is difficult to imagine what America would be like today without Thomas Jefferson's amazing contributions. In addition to drafting the Declaration of Independence, Jefferson was America's third president, a scientist, an inventor, a farmer who introduced new plants and farming techniques to the country, the mastermind behind the Louisiana Purchase, a radical political thinker, the country's first **secretary of state**, a legal scholar, the founder of the University of Virginia, and an architect whose contributions are still remembered today.

In 1962, President John F. Kennedy invited a group of winners of the Nobel Prize, the most esteemed award in science, mathematics, and the humanities, to dinner at the White House. Welcoming them, he said, "I think this is the most extraordinary collection of talent, of human knowledge, that has ever been gathered at the White House, with the possible exception of when Thomas Jefferson dined alone."

CHAPTER 1

A Hungry Mind

Life, Liberty, and the pursuit of Happiness

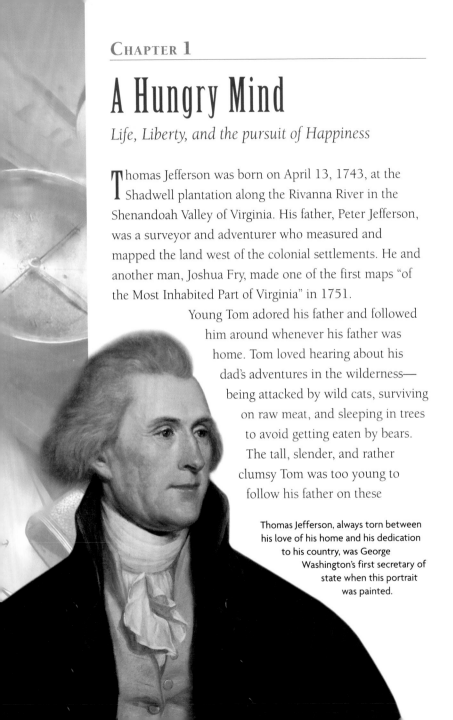

Thomas Jefferson was born on April 13, 1743, at the Shadwell plantation along the Rivanna River in the Shenandoah Valley of Virginia. His father, Peter Jefferson, was a surveyor and adventurer who measured and mapped the land west of the colonial settlements. He and another man, Joshua Fry, made one of the first maps "of the Most Inhabited Part of Virginia" in 1751.

Young Tom adored his father and followed him around whenever his father was home. Tom loved hearing about his dad's adventures in the wilderness— being attacked by wild cats, surviving on raw meat, and sleeping in trees to avoid getting eaten by bears. The tall, slender, and rather clumsy Tom was too young to follow his father on these

Thomas Jefferson, always torn between his love of his home and his dedication to his country, was George Washington's first secretary of state when this portrait was painted.

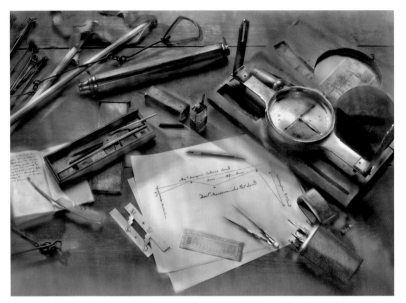

Peter Jefferson's surveying equipment allowed him to map the colony of Virginia. Young Tom learned his love of mathematics, design, and the wilderness from his father.

journeys, but he wanted nothing more than to be just like him.

In the mornings when Peter Jefferson was home, he taught Tom to hunt and fish, and in the evenings, sitting by the fire, he taught his son mathematics and allowed him to look through his well-worn books. Jefferson family legend says that Tom had read all the books in his father's library by the time he was five years old.

As his father traveled around to visit his farms, Tom would often ride alongside him with a book tucked inside his coat pocket. He especially loved to climb the rugged path to a hilltop on his family's property—he could see for miles. The place seemed enchanted to Tom. When he was grown, he named it Monticello, which means "little mountain" in Italian, and built his home there.

The hilltop that Jefferson named Monticello offered a breathtaking view of Virginia's Shenandoah Valley. He often rode there to read and think, long before he built his famous home there.

A colonel in the colonial militia, or volunteer army, Peter Jefferson traveled to the outer reaches of the colony and spoke with many Indians. As Indian leaders traveled from their settlements to Williamsburg, the capital of the colony, to meet with colonial governors, they often would pay their respects to Colonel Jefferson. Outacity, the famous chief of the Cherokees, and 165 others of his tribe visited the Jefferson family on one such journey. Tom was awed by the great chief and was fascinated by Indians throughout his life.

Peter Jefferson never went to school, but he wanted to make certain that his oldest son did. When Tom was nine, he rode more than fifty miles away to study with the Reverend William

Douglas at Dover Church. Tom and other students lived at the school for months at a time. Like many students, Tom complained about the terrible food there and made fun of his teacher. He also learned to dance the minuets and country dances that young gentlemen were required to know. Around this time, he learned to play the violin and became passionate about playing. He especially loved to play with his older sister Jane, who played the harpsichord and sang.

Without a Friend

When Tom was fourteen, his big, strong, and seemingly immortal father suddenly died. Tom was devastated. Although his mother was alive and he had two beloved older sisters and

Peter Jefferson: A Life of Service

Peter Jefferson taught his son the importance of community service by example. When Albemarle County, Virginia, was formed in 1744, Peter Jefferson became justice of the peace and judge of the **court of chancery**—a position given to men respected by others for their fairness, even though they had no formal legal training. He also served as sheriff when Tom was a boy, and in the House of Burgesses, the lawmaking body of the colony. Peter Jefferson was also a devoted friend. When his best friend, William Randolph, died in 1745, Jefferson moved with his family fifty miles east to take over Tuckahoe, Randolph's plantation, and care for Randolph's orphaned children. For the next seven years, the Jeffersons and the Randolphs lived together. The children attended a one-room schoolhouse on the farm, where young Tom's formal education began.

four younger sisters and a brother, he felt abandoned. His father had been his hero, and he was furious to have him snatched away. No one could help Tom feel less angry. He escaped into his books and music.

Six months after his father's death, Tom returned to school, but closer to Shadwell. Already nearly six feet two inches tall, with freckled skin and red hair, Tom and his father's servant Sawney rode on horseback fourteen miles to a small boarding school in the home of Reverend James Maury. Reverend Maury, a father of eight children, was a father figure to Tom during these years.

It was Reverend Maury who taught Tom to love language. Tom read Latin and Greek texts and learned modern French well enough to read the great French thinkers of the age. Reverend

Virginia's Rivanna River ran near the Shadwell plantation, Thomas Jefferson's childhood home. He learned to hunt and fish nearby.

Music: A Sweet Companion

Thomas Jefferson loved music. He learned to play the violin as a boy, and he played for many hours as his sister Jane sang. His family could often hear him humming or softly singing to himself as he worked or rode his horse. "Do not neglect your music," he later wrote to his daughter Patsy. "It will be a companion which will sweeten many hours of life to you."

As a boy, Thomas Jefferson learned to play the violin and to read music. When his family home burned to the ground, servants saved his beloved "fiddle."

Maury also taught him science, or "natural philosophy," as it was then called. They rode together to the Blue Ridge Mountains to learn about rocks and the blueprint of the past that was hidden inside them. Many years later, Tom said that his two years with the Maury family and the other students were among the happiest of his life.

When Tom was fifteen, Reverend Maury knew he had taught him all he could and that it was time for his young student to head to college. The first choice for Virginia gentlemen was the College of William and Mary in Williamsburg.

College of William and Mary

In March 1760, Tom and his personal servant, Jupiter, rode 150 miles through the forests of Virginia to Williamsburg. Williamsburg was the capital of the colony and it was, by far, the

Thomas Jefferson lived in the Wren Building (center) during his first year at the College of William and Mary. He worked hard there, often studying fifteen hours a day.

biggest city he had ever seen. He arrived there during the meetings of the House of Burgesses, the lawmaking body of the colony and the oldest representative government body in the **colonies**. The city was teeming with representatives from around Virginia, and fancy-dress balls and dinners occurred every night. Tom had never seen anything like it.

A few weeks later was race week, when the best horses from Virginia's richest plantations would compete, and wealthy men and students would wager on the outcome. Tom loved watching the fine horses running, but he had little interest in betting on horses—or on cards or dice. He did enjoy gathering with the other students at Raleigh Tavern, though, where young men and women would dance and drink and flirt with each other.

Jefferson's teacher of mathematics, science, and philosophy was Dr. William Small. An inspiring lecturer, Dr. Small also became Tom's friend. They spent countless hours together talking, dining, and arguing. Dr. Small introduced Tom to writers and ideas that would influence his thinking throughout his life.

Few students worked harder than Tom. He "could tear himself away from his dearest friends to fly to his studies," joked his friend John Page. Tom studied and read by candlelight until well after midnight. His roommate, John Tyler, whose future son John would later become president, was also a serious student, and the two would read, study, and play their violins together. To keep fit, Tom liked to run, hike, and swim, and every morning he bathed his feet in ice-cold water, which he thought kept him from catching colds. He continued that habit throughout his life.

Dr. Small introduced Tom to writers and ideas that would influence his thinking throughout his life.

Although rather serious and bookish, Tom had friends at the college who would often drag him to dances, plays, concerts, weddings, and local taverns. His visits home between terms

College of William and Mary

The college Thomas Jefferson attended was founded in 1693 by England's King William III and Queen Mary II. It is the second oldest college in the U.S., after Harvard. Money to open the college came, in part, from a British tax imposed on tobacco exports from Virginia and Maryland, just the sort of taxation without representation Jefferson would later oppose. Six other signers of the Declaration of Independence also graduated from the College of William and Mary.

seemed dull and boring in comparison to life in Williamsburg. He would escape the tedious happenings of country life by paddling his canoe across the nearby Rivanna River and trudging up to the top of the hill he had loved to visit with his father. There, Tom would daydream about the house he would soon build.

A Legal Education

In 1762, when Tom was nineteen and his years at William and Mary were coming to an end, he decided to study law. There were no law schools at that time. Instead, law students studied under practicing lawyers and then took an examination. Dr. Small knew the perfect teacher for Tom: his good friend George Wythe. Over the next several years, Wythe took the hardworking, gifted student under his wing and became Tom's guide through law studies and a lifelong friend. Wythe later became a signer of the Declaration of Independence and America's first professor of law.

Jefferson spent many evenings over dinners of oysters, wild duck, and Virginia ham at the Governor's Palace with Small and Wythe. They were the guests of Francis Fauquier, the

George Wythe taught Thomas Jefferson the law and became a lifelong friend. Wythe was a brilliant lawyer who left his entire legal library to Jefferson when he died.

talented and rather mysterious royal lieutenant governor of the colony. It was gossiped that he had lost his family fortune gambling, but Jefferson considered him to be "the ablest man who had ever filled that office." During those dinner conversations, Jefferson later remembered, he heard "more good sense, more rational and philosophical conversation than in all my life besides."

By the time he had finished his legal training, Tom was one of the most knowledgeable men in the colonies. Although he was a brilliant student, he was shy and awkward around girls. At nineteen he had a crush on a girl named Rebecca Burwell. After more than a year of admiring Rebecca from afar, he finally danced with her. He had practiced for weeks what he would say to her, but when he finally held her in his arms, he was tongue-tied. She smiled politely at the end of the dance and returned to her friends. Mortified, he left the dance shortly afterward. A few months later, she became engaged to another man.

By the time he had finished his legal training, Tom was one of the most knowledgeable men in the colonies. Although he was a brilliant student, he was shy and awkward around girls.

Tom's heart was broken, but his mind was soon on other things. While he had been studying law, Britain had begun to tax the colonies to help pay for the added troops needed to protect the colonies in the **French and Indian War**. Williamsburg soon became a center of polite but firm refusal to pay the tax, and Tom soon became a leader in the rebellion.

CHAPTER 2

Inching Toward Liberty

Under the law of nature, all men are born free.

In June 1765, Jefferson headed home to Shadwell to study for the bar exam, which would permit him to practice law. He also spent countless hours reading books by influential political thinkers. He had plenty of time to do both.

In 1765, Parliament passed the Stamp Act, which taxed every piece of printed paper that the colonists used, from official government licenses to playing cards. The tax was supposed to raise money to support the troops England had sent to protect the colonies. While the tax itself was small, the colonists were concerned that this was the first of many such taxes that would be imposed on them without their consent.

Colonists displayed their hatred of the Stamp Act in boycotts, in riots, and even on teapots.

When the Virginia **Assembly** passed resolutions protesting the Stamp Act, the royal governor was so furious that he shut down the Assembly. Lawyers in Virginia protested, too. They refused to use the tax stamps that they had to put on legal documents, and thus closed down the courts. For an entire year, Jefferson could not practice law or take the bar exam. Instead, he threw himself into making plans for a home of his own.

The First Monticello

When Jefferson turned twenty-one in 1764, he received his inheritance from his father's will. He was allowed to choose several pieces of farmland from his father's holdings around Virginia. One of these was the "little mountain" that he had loved since childhood.

Jefferson's vast lands offered him some practical and beautiful spots for building a home. Most men would have chosen to build along the Rivanna River, which ran through the region and offered easy access to ports for shipping crops and a ready supply of water. But Jefferson was not like most men. He was a dreamer, and he had the money to make his dreams come true. He began sketching plans for a home on the mountaintop.

This early sketch of Monticello, drawn by Jefferson in 1769–70, is a rare look at the first Monticello, which was later redesigned and rebuilt with its familiar dome.

The House of Burgesses

In 1766, after Parliament withdrew the Stamp Act, the courts reopened, and Jefferson was admitted to the bar of the Virginia General Court. As he rode throughout the colony while working on his cases, he soon became the man whom other lawyers hired when they needed a lawyer. Word spread that he was a man who won his cases.

In December 1768, in the first election after Jefferson had completed his law studies, he was elected to the Virginia House of Burgesses representing Albemarle County—the seat once held by his father. Elections in those days were simpler—and the number of voters was more limited—than today. Only men who owned fifty acres of land without buildings on them, a farm of at least twenty-five acres with a house, or a house or lot in town were able to vote.

On an evening in mid-December, the voters gathered at the courthouse in Charlottesville for rum, cakes, and lots of handshaking and backslapping. Jefferson was running against Edward Carter, a powerful landowner who then held the seat. The candidates shared the cost of the rum and cakes. After each of the voters called out his choice at the end of the evening, Jefferson had won, launching his career in politics.

The following April, Jefferson was again riding across the state to Williamsburg, this time to take part in the Virginia House of Burgesses. George Washington also served as a member.

Tension was in the air in Williamsburg. Although the Stamp Act had been repealed by Parliament, a new set of laws limited the colonists' rights to a trial by their peers.

Tension was in the air in Williamsburg. Although the Stamp Act had been repealed by Parliament, a new set of laws limited the colonists' rights to a trial by their peers. The House of Burgesses signed more resolutions in protest. Lord Botetourt, Virginia's new royal governor, was so upset that, as the royal governor before him had done, he dissolved the Assembly.

But the now-former members of the House of Burgesses would have none of it. Jefferson and the others marched down Duke of Gloucester Street to the Raleigh Tavern and voted to boycott all British goods in protest. The list of banned goods was long, and included everything from slaves to watches and leather goods. Thomas Jefferson was the sixteenth of the representatives to sign the agreement. In his first session as a politician, he was already considered an enemy of the king.

RUN away from the subscriber in *Albemarle*, a Mulatto slave called *Sandy*, about 35 years of age, his stature is rather low, inclining to corpulence, and his complexion light; he is a shoemaker by trade, in which he uses his left hand principally, can do coarse carpenters work, and is something of a horse jockey; he is greatly addicted to drink, and when drunk is insolent and disorderly, in his conversation he swears much, and in his behaviour is artful and knavish. He took with him a white horse, much scarred with traces, of which it is expected he will endeavour to dispose; he also carried his shoemakers tools, and will probably endeavour to get employment that way. Whoever conveys the said slave to me, in *Albemarle*, shall have 40 s. reward, if taken up within the county, 4 l. if elsewhere within the colony, and 10 l. if in any other colony, from

THOMAS JEFFERSON.

This newspaper ad seeking the return of a runaway slave was placed by Jefferson in 1769. After the "troublemaker" was returned, Jefferson sold him to another slaveholder.

All Men Are Born Free

When the Assembly was not in session, Jefferson continued practicing law. He was a very busy lawyer, handling more than one hundred cases each year. One of his cases was important in establishing the **separation of church and state**, which would later become a cornerstone of the United States **Constitution**.

Jefferson also struggled with the question of slavery. Although his family had held slaves his whole life, he questioned whether any man had the right to own another. During his first session in the House of Burgesses, he tried to pass a law that would have made it easy for a slave owner to free a slave simply by registering in the county court. The Assembly quickly voted it down.

He spoke out against slavery in several public forums, calling it evil, but he relied on slaves to work on his own plantations. He once handled a legal case, free of charge, for a slave trying to win his freedom. In that case, Jefferson said to the judges of the General Court, "Under the law of nature, all men are born free." Unfortunately, he did not convince the judges. In fact, the chief judge banged his gavel right after Jefferson finished speaking and ruled in favor of the slave owner—even before the slave owner's lawyer spoke.

Jefferson would remain torn about slavery throughout his life. He knew slavery was immoral, but he was unwilling or unable to confront his family, friends, and fellow lawmakers—or himself—to change this institution.

Monticello Construction Begins

Despite his busy law practice and constant traveling, Jefferson continued building a home of his own. Working from plans that Jefferson had drawn, builders started construction in 1769 on a small, one-room building that would later become the south pavilion of the estate. The work sped up the following year, when tragedy struck at Shadwell.

In February, as Jefferson was conducting some business in nearby Charlottesville, a family slave rushed into the room. He told Jefferson that his family home had burned to the ground but that no one had been hurt. His mother, sisters, and brothers were safely crowded into one of the other buildings on the property.

Jefferson soon rented rooms in Charlottesville while the rest of his family went to live with his uncle nearby. Now more than ever, he wanted a place of his own, and he hired more construction workers to make bricks and finish the one-room building that he would call home while the rest of his house was built. He moved in during the fall of that year.

Thomas Jefferson Falls in Love

In his travels as a lawyer, Jefferson would visit old friends from Reverend Maury's school and from William and Mary. He would bring news from other friends, the latest gossip from Williamsburg, and a bag filled with chess pieces. His friends would provide dinner, a bed, and a chessboard. During the five years that he had been studying law, many of his schoolmates had married and were starting families of their own. His old friend Dabney Carr had married Jefferson's sister Martha and happily settled down to practice law.

Jefferson, whose life had always been filled with his beloved books, realized that he was missing something important: someone with whom he could share his life. Soon he found a perfect match. Martha Wayles Skelton, called "Patty" by all who knew her, was beautiful, with dark hair and hazel eyes. She was also intelligent and better educated than most colonial women. She loved to read books, sing, and play the harpsichord.

For nearly two years, Jefferson visited The Forest, Patty's father's plantation, hoping to convince her to marry him. Thomas

Martha "Patty" Wayles Skelton Jefferson: "A Gentle and Amiable Wife"

Patty was Jefferson's devoted companion. Isaac, a family slave, remembered her coming out to the kitchen "with a cookery book in her hand," reading recipes to his mother, Ursula, for the cakes and tarts that Jefferson loved. Patty and Jefferson spent many evenings together reading aloud and playing duets. When she was dying in 1782, she is said to have asked Jefferson never to marry again. He never did.

Tom and Patty Jefferson shared the tiny one-room South Pavilion for nearly two years and Patty gave birth to their daughter Patsy there while Monticello was under construction.

Jefferson and Martha "Patty" Wayles Skelton were married on New Year's Day 1772 at The Forest. A few weeks later they began a journey of about one hundred miles to Jefferson's one-room quarters at Monticello, which they would now share. The room, an eighteen-foot square, served them "for parlor, for kitchen, and hall. I might add, for bedchamber and study too," Jefferson wrote to a friend. For three months the young married couple enjoyed a quiet life together there as work on the main house continued.

Nurseries of Revolution

In March 1773, their idyllic world came to an end. Virginia's new royal governor, Lord Dunmore, called the Virginia Assembly in for a session. He wanted the lawmakers to raise taxes to support the College of William and Mary and to renovate the Governor's Palace. Little did he know that Jefferson and other radical colleagues had something else in mind.

Jefferson wrote a resolution setting up "committees of correspondence" to communicate regularly with the other colonies, sharing news and strategies for rebellion. The resolution passed unanimously. Britain discouraged such official communication between colonies, because it wanted each colony to remain separate.

The royal governor, however, failed to see the power that the colonies would wield if they worked together, and he did nothing to stop it. Soon, Jefferson and the others were meeting regularly at the Raleigh Tavern, plotting protests against the British and writing to like-minded men throughout the other colonies. Within months nearly every colony had similar committees of correspondence. These committees would soon become nurseries of revolution.

Later that same year, the British repealed all the taxes on colonies except for a small tax on tea. The British allowed the East India Company to sell their extra tea at such low prices that they thought the colonists would not care about the tax. But radicals in Boston, Massachusetts, led by Samuel Adams, refused to allow the tea to be unloaded from the

In protest one evening, they dressed as American Indian warriors and dumped hundreds of chests of tea overboard. Today that event is known as the Boston Tea Party.

The tactics of royal governor John Murray, Lord Dunmore, here wearing his Scottish family tartan, gave Virginia patriots plenty to protest in the years leading up to the American Revolution.

ships in Boston harbor. In protest one evening, they dressed as American Indian warriors and dumped hundreds of chests of tea overboard. Today that event is known as the Boston Tea Party.

King George III was so angry when he heard about the protest that he imposed a military-run government on Massachusetts. Virginia lawmakers reasoned that if the people of Massachusetts could have their rights stripped away, then the same thing could happen to any colonists. The lawmakers voted to call for a **Continental Congress** to bring representatives from all the colonies to Philadelphia in the fall of 1774, where they could decide together what to do about the "Intolerable Acts," as Britain's actions against Massachusetts came to be called.

Jefferson wrote instructions for the Virginia **delegates** to the Congress, but his suggestions were believed by some to be too radical and were voted down by his colleagues. Others thought his words were so powerful that they had them printed in a pamphlet that soon found its way to the other colonies and across the ocean to England. In his essay, "A Summary View of the Rights of British America," Jefferson argued that colonists were entitled to the same rights as British citizens. More shocking to the British, though, was his claim that "kings are the servants, not the proprietors of the people." This pamphlet, Jefferson's first political document, would help shape the American Revolution.

King George III ruled Great Britain from 1760 to 1820. Although most colonists felt loyal to him, they wanted a voice in making the laws under which they lived.

CHAPTER 3

Declaring Independence

An expression of the American mind.

In 1774 the Continental Congress outlined the rights of colonists to "life, liberty and property" and imposed a boycott of British goods until Parliament repealed its taxes and ended the strong-arm tactics that stripped colonists of those rights. Congress decided to reconvene the following year if the changes were not made. By 1775 the situation had worsened and tensions were so high that some colonists were calling for a formal break with Britain.

Patrick Henry delivers his protest against the Stamp Act in 1775 urging Virginians to take up arms against the British.

Patrick Henry: Inspiring Revolution

Patrick Henry's fiery "give me liberty or give me death" speech in 1775 roused the Virginia Assembly to become the first colonial government to propose armed revolt against the British. He helped write Virginia's first constitution and served as Virginia's first elected governor.

In March 1775, Patrick Henry roused the delegates to the second Virginia Convention, a meeting in preparation for the Second Continental Congress. He made a passionate speech urging Virginians to form **militias** to defend themselves against the English before it was too late. When the secret votes were counted, sixty-five were in favor and sixty were against. Henry's resolution passed, but barely. In Virginia, as in many of the colonies, opinion was split about raising arms against England.

After taking this decisive step toward armed conflict with Britain, the convention members elected their representatives to the Second Continental Congress, to be held later in the spring. Jefferson, who at thirty-two was one of the youngest in the Assembly, was chosen as an alternate in case Peyton Randolph, president of the Virginia Convention, was needed in Virginia during the congressional session in Philadelphia.

After the convention, Jefferson returned home to Patty and their daughters, Patsy and Jane. Jefferson's home was finally livable. The library, parlor for entertaining, drawing room (similar to a family room), dining room, and master bedroom were complete, while work continued on the rest of the house. He loved living in the sawdust and disarray of a construction site. When a section did not turn out as he had imagined, or the builders confronted an unexpected problem, he would have them take apart whatever they had built and do it again.

He was content to remain at Monticello, but the times demanded that he choose his country over his comfort. In June 1775, Peyton Randolph was called back to Virginia to handle the rising tensions with the royal governor, Lord Dunmore. Jefferson had to replace Randolph at the Second Continental Congress. He hated to leave his family, and he worried about Patty, whose health was frail.

On to Philadelphia

Two days after Jefferson arrived in Philadelphia, a courier galloped into town late at night with sobering news of the Battle of Breeds Hill. In a daylong battle between Boston **patriots** and British soldiers, 20 percent of the patriots were killed or wounded. British soldiers, known as Redcoats because of the color of their uniforms, suffered casualties of a staggering 40 percent.

Massachusetts delegates John Adams, Samuel Adams, and John Hancock awoke the other representatives with the news. Jefferson and the other bleary-eyed delegates gathered at the State House in the middle of the night to vote on sending soldiers and gunpowder to aid the patriots. Jefferson believed that the time for negotiations with the British had passed. There was no "prospect of accommodation" except by the "interposition of arms," he wrote to a friend.

Jefferson was thrown into the business of Congress with little formal introduction. The delegates from the other colonies were curious about this red-haired man whose reputation as a fiery writer had preceded him. But Jefferson was quiet during the

A Bloody Beginning

The Battle of Breeds Hill, more commonly called the Battle of Bunker Hill, was the first major clash of the American Revolution. On June 17, 1775, troops from throughout New England gathered outside of Boston to confront British soldiers. The fighting was fierce. Although the British eventually won, seizing the rebel position at the top of Breeds Hill, they suffered more than twice as many casualties, about 1,000, as the Americans, whose dead numbered around 450. In a single day, the American Revolution had been transformed from a war of words to a bloody battle.

The British victory was short lived. General George Washington arrived two weeks later to take control of the American troops. By the following spring, he had forced the British to flee Boston. The Revolutionary War would continue for eight years.

British troops are attacked by patriot gunfire in this painting of the Battle of Breeds Hill. Although the British won, their high casualties inspired the patriots to continue fighting.

sometimes raucous meetings, preferring to observe in the larger forum and speak his piece in smaller gatherings. John Adams wrote about Jefferson that, "During the whole time I sat with him in Congress, I never heard him utter three sentences together." But, Adams added, Jefferson "was so prompt, frank, explicit, and decisive upon committees and in conversation . . . that he soon seized upon my heart." The tall, slender Virginian and the short, stocky New Englander often spent time talking quietly together, and became devoted friends.

Jefferson's six weeks attending the Congress in Philadelphia were hot, muggy, and fly infested. The conditions during meetings were even worse because the windows of the State House, now known as Independence Hall, were kept closed at all times to prevent the city's loyalists, those who sided with the British, from listening in on the discussions.

On August 1, 1775, Congress adjourned for a brief time and Jefferson rushed back to Monticello. He arrived home to tragedy. His younger daughter, Jane, died before she was eighteen months old. In those times before immunizations and antibiotics, many children did not survive to adulthood. He buried her in the family graveyard near her namesake, his beloved sister Jane, who had died ten years before. He delayed returning to Philadelphia for as long as he could, but in the end he had to tear himself away from his grieving wife.

Blood Spilled in Virginia

That fall, Jefferson returned to Philadelphia with a servant and boarded with the cabinetmaker Benjamin Randolph in a house just a short walk away from the State House. The news from Virginia was ominous. In November, Royal Governor Lord

Philadelphia's State House, now known as Independence Hall, was the site of the Second Continental Congress, where the Declaration of Independence was debated in the summer of 1776.

Dunmore declared **martial law**, giving the British military power over the government.

The Virginia militia learned that the British were planning an attack on Norfolk, the colony's most important port. On December 8, the militia, along with volunteers from North Carolina, confronted British soldiers there. Within minutes, 102 British men had been injured or killed. Only one militiaman was slightly hurt. The first Southern battle of the American Revolution ended in an American victory, but the fighting had just begun.

The Virginia militia learned that the British were planning an attack on Norfolk, the colony's most important port. On December 8, the militia, along with volunteers from North Carolina, confronted British soldiers there.

Hearing the news in Philadelphia, Jefferson rushed home to make certain that Patty and Patsy were safe. He tried to live there quietly over the next few months, away from both politics and war. Patty had been weak since the birth of their daughter Jane, and she seemed worse whenever Jefferson was away.

Then, in March, Jefferson's mother died suddenly. The strain took a heavy toll on him. He suffered from a very painful migraine headache that kept him in bed in a darkened room for nearly five weeks. Throughout much of his life, he would continue to suffer from these unbearable headaches when tensions were high.

Free and Independent States

Jefferson returned to Philadelphia in May 1776. To have more privacy and some relief from Philadelphia's relentless summer heat, Jefferson moved to a two-story house on the edge of town owned by Jacob Graff, a German bricklayer. Jefferson rented a bedroom and a parlor on the second floor, which offered him sunlight and pleasant breezes while he worked. He brought along his favorite Windsor chair and a portable desk built to his specifications by his former landlord, Benjamin Randolph.

Just as Jefferson was arriving in Philadelphia, his former colleagues in the House of Burgesses were assembling in Williamsburg for another Virginia Convention. They declared Virginia independent and began plans for a new government. They also resolved unanimously that Virginia's delegates to the Continental Congress should "declare the United Colonies free and independent states absolved from all allegiance to or

Jefferson wrote the Declaration of Independence on the second floor of Jacob Graff's house, where he and his servants lived while he served in the Second Continental Congress.

dependence upon the Crown or Parliament of Great Britain." They were the first colony to call for independence.

On May 27, 1776, the Virginia delegation presented their resolution to John Hancock, the president of the Congress. Two weeks would pass before Congress opened debate on the subject of independence. Finally, on June 7, 1776, Richard Henry Lee, one of Jefferson's fellow delegates from Virginia, formally proposed before the entire Continental Congress the resolution that "these united colonies are, and of right ought to be, free and independent states."

The debate began the following morning. Jefferson and others quickly realized that the middle colonies (New York, New Jersey, Pennsylvania, Delaware, and Maryland) and South Carolina were "not yet matured for falling from the parent stem, but they were fast advancing to that state." The Congress decided to postpone a final vote until July 1 so that the delegates could get further instructions from their colonies.

The Declaration of Independence

In the meantime, on June 11, Congress established a committee to write a Declaration of Independence that would spell out the reasons for the decision, once the vote was final. The committee was made up of Jefferson, John Adams (Massachusetts), Benjamin Franklin (Pennsylvania), Roger Sherman (Connecticut), and Robert Livingston (New York). They met in Franklin's rooms, since he was laid up with a painful episode of gout. They discussed briefly what the document should say and chose Jefferson to write it.

From June 13 to June 28, Jefferson spent all his time, when not attending Congressional meetings, sitting in his bright, airy

Thomas Jefferson (left) reviews his draft of the Declaration of Independence with committee members John Adams, Benjamin Franklin, Robert Livingston, and Roger Sherman.

rooms at his portable desk and drafting the Declaration of Independence. The task he had been given, he later said, was "to place before mankind the common sense of the subject," to spell out, for all the world, the reasons why the colonies had to take the drastic step of declaring independence from Britain. Equally important, the Declaration was to explain the ideals on which this new country would be founded. When it was finished, the committee made only minor changes.

The Declaration of Independence was submitted to the Congress on June 28. But before it could be considered,

Jefferson wrote the Declaration of Independence on this mahogany lap desk. The drawer held pens and ink, and the surface could be raised to a comfortable angle for writing.

Congress had to vote on the resolution to declare independence. The resolution passed on July 2. Then, after relatively little discussion on whether to declare independence, the Congress members began three days of torturous debate on the language of the document declaring it. Jefferson suffered silently as every idea, every phrase, every word was discussed and often changed, or completely cut. Benjamin Franklin, who sat next to him, could see that his young colleague was in agony and tried to reassure and amuse him. Jefferson smiled feebly at his friend's stories, all the while feeling as though someone were cutting out his heart.

In the end, the omissions bothered Jefferson the most. Congress completely removed his condemnation of the slave trade. It also cut the phrases that blamed not only the king but

Home of the Declaration of Independence

In May 1776 Thomas Jefferson moved to the outskirts of Philadelphia to escape the excessive heat of the city. He rented two large and well-lit rooms on the second floor of Jacob Graff's home. The cooling breezes that wafted through the big windows brought hundreds of horseflies from a nearby stable, which plagued Jefferson as he wrote the Declaration of Independence. The house was demolished in 1883 and then rebuilt in 1975.

Thomas Jefferson drafted the Declaration of Independence in his airy parlor. He wrote on his portable desk placed on a table.

the people of Britain for the state the colonies were in. Even years later, he complained that Congress balked "lest they should give [the British] offense," at a time when British and American blood was already being shed.

Finally, on the evening of July 4, 1776, the Continental

"We Hold These Truths…"

The Declaration of Independence was written to explain to the world why the American colonies had decided to break from Great Britain. In the words of its primary author, Thomas Jefferson, it was also intended to be "an expression of the American mind."

More than two hundred years later, it remains the simplest explanation of what was then a radical idea: "We hold these truths to be self-evident, that all men are created equal, that they are endowed by their Creator with certain unalienable Rights, that among these are Life, Liberty, and the pursuit of Happiness."

Even more radical, in an age of kings and tyrants, was the Declaration's insistence that a government's power comes not from God but from the consent of the governed. If a government fails to support "Life, Liberty, and the pursuit of Happiness," citizens have every right to establish a new government.

The Declaration of Independence defined a nation and explained a new philosophy of government. It has inspired countless **democracies** that have followed in the time since that sultry Philadelphia summer of 1776.

Congress approved the Declaration of Independence, and John Hancock, president of the Congress, and Charles Thomson, secretary, signed it, making it official. Copies were printed and sent to all the state committees and to General George Washington to read to his troops. The rest of the Congress signed it weeks later.

On July 8, as crowds cheered, the Declaration of Independence was read aloud in public for the first time by the sheriff of Philadelphia County. Jefferson, still smarting from the changes made to it, may not even have been there. Only years later was he publicly identified as the author of this most important expression of American ideals.

John Adams, Roger Sherman, Robert Livingston, Thomas Jefferson, and Benjamin Franklin present their document to the Continental Congress in this famous painting by John Trumball.

The Declaration of Independence was adopted on July 4, 1776. It was later copied on parchment and signed by the members of Congress.

CHAPTER 4

A Governor Under Siege

[He confessed that he was unprepared by his] line of life and education for the command of armies.

T homas Jefferson returned to his waiting wife and daughter in September 1776. He had promised Patty that he would not leave her again, but the new Virginia Assembly was meeting in Williamsburg and it needed his talents to help form a new state government. The constitution that had been passed by the Assembly, while Jefferson served in the Continental Congress, was too

In the fall of 1776, Thomas, Patty, and Patsy Jefferson rode in a carriage like this one to Williamsburg, Virginia's capital, where Jefferson helped shape the state's new government.

conservative for Jefferson's radical thinking. A new state needed a new vision—his vision—and the time was now, while revolution was in the air.

In October, he packed up Patty and Patsy, wagonloads of belongings, and several slaves to care for them all, and began the bumpy, weeklong, 150-mile ride east from Monticello to Williamsburg. They moved into the home of George Wythe, his old law teacher and friend, who was then in Philadelphia at the Continental Congress.

In those early years of the republic, Jefferson wrote more than one hundred laws on subjects ranging from religious freedom to public education. He soon learned, though, that having a vision for a government and running a government were two different things. During the next five years, he would experience some of his happiest moments, and certainly some of his lowest, while serving his country.

Crimes and Punishments

That fall, Jefferson was asked to chair a committee to revise the laws of Virginia. The project would take him nearly three years. Jefferson and his family soon returned to Monticello, where he kept one of the finest law libraries in Virginia. He needed the books for his research. His wife and daughter were happy to be going home.

Jefferson would rise at dawn each morning and record the temperature in a notebook, as he did every morning throughout most of his life. He worked in his study through much of the day, spending countless hours reviewing the laws of Britain and the ancient civilizations, and shaping them to better reflect the values of the new republic. He made the laws of Virginia easier to

A page from Jefferson's handwritten draft bill for reforming Virginia's laws on capital crimes, which are those punishable by death.

understand and identified punishments that fit the crimes better than they had in the laws of Britain.

In May 1777, Jefferson's only son was born, but he died after only a few weeks. Happily, the following year Patty gave birth to another baby, a girl whom they named Mary, and who was healthy, strong, and as beautiful as her mother. Mary, nicknamed "Polly," would survive to adulthood.

By the spring of 1779, Jefferson had finished his work helping to revise Virginia's laws. He told his friend Edmund Pendleton that he was thinking of resigning from the House of Delegates and retiring to Monticello to farm, write, and enjoy his family.

Inventing America

Thomas Jefferson, in a very real sense, invented the United States during his years in Virginia's House of Delegates. The laws he wrote for Virginia became models for the United States government. Some of the important bills that he introduced involved:

Property rights: He helped eliminate colonial laws that caused land to pass automatically to the oldest sons through many generations. These laws, which allowed restrictions on the sale of inherited land, had created a small group of very powerful families in Virginia who owned much of the land. Under the new laws, Jefferson envisioned a society in which the best men could rise to power and wealth, regardless of what family they came from.

Religious freedom: The Episcopal Church, as the Church of England was known in the colonies, had been the official state religion. Jefferson was instrumental in removing its official status and giving people of other religions the right to worship as they chose. He believed that religion was not the business of government. Jefferson's Statute for Religious Freedom was one of the achievements of which he was most proud.

Public education: According to Jefferson, a republic could thrive only with well-educated citizens. He believed in an "aristocracy of virtue and talent," proposing that all children receive free schooling to learn how to read and write. The best students, regardless of wealth, would be selected to continue to the College of William and Mary to be educated, boarded, and clothed at state expense for three years.

Governor Jefferson

Despite Jefferson's mixed feelings about politics, the Assembly chose him as Virginia's second governor in June 1779. In those days the Assembly members, all men, were chosen by landowners in their districts, and they in turn chose the governor. Again the family moved to Williamsburg. They would live in the Governor's Palace, where Jefferson had spent so many happy evenings in lively conversation as a student. But unlike the British royal governors who once lived there, Jefferson had very little authority. Under the new constitution, the Assembly—the State Senate and the House of Delegates—held nearly all the power to make decisions. The governor had to ask permission of the Council of State, made up of eight Assembly members, before he could do anything of importance. Jefferson felt powerless even from the beginning.

Jefferson and the Assembly realized that Virginia's government was vulnerable to attack since it was located in a capital on the coast, where British ships were a constant threat. In April 1780, Jefferson and his family moved eighty miles inland to the new capital, Richmond.

War Comes to Virginia

As the year wore on, the Revolutionary War shifted to the South. Charleston, South Carolina, was the scene of a bloody battle, and British sailors regularly raided Virginia coastal towns for supplies. In December 1780, a fleet of British ships commanded by colonial traitor Benedict Arnold, a former colonial officer under George Washington, entered the Chesapeake Bay. Arnold was headed up the James River toward Richmond, determined to destroy Virginia's meager weapons factory and bring back a prize: Thomas Jefferson himself.

Originally the home of colonial Virginia's royal governors sent from England, the Governor's Palace in Williamsburg became Jefferson's home when he was chosen as the state's second governor in 1779.

On New Year's Eve morning, a messenger galloped up to the governor's house. He ran up to the door, where he told the governor that twenty-seven ships had been seen entering the bay two days earlier. Jefferson hoped they were the French reinforcements that the patriots had long been hoping for.

If the fleet was British, he assumed it was stopping simply to raid for provisions on the way to the fighting in South Carolina. Jefferson decided not to notify the Assembly or call up the militia until he knew more. He did not want to cry wolf and risk that the militia might not show up when they would really be needed.

Two days later, on January 2, 1781, he learned that the fleet was British and that it had reached Williamsburg on New Year's

Eve. He quickly informed the Assembly and called up the militia from nearby counties, but he had lost two precious days in waiting. The enemy was at the door. On January 4 he was awakened to learn that the ships were headed straight up the James River for Richmond.

Over the next two days and nights, Jefferson seemed to be everywhere at once, supervising the movement of guns and ammunition out of the city so they would not be destroyed, and helping evacuate people, including his own family. As he moved along, he rode frantically in search of Colonel von Steuben, head of the Continental Army in Virginia. Jefferson hoped von Steuben would have a strategy for saving the city, but he knew that they had neither enough men nor guns to fight the British. All they could do was leave the city. When the British entered Richmond, Jefferson and the Council of State were nowhere to be found.

British soldiers may not have found Jefferson, but they did find his house. They stole many valuables and important government papers and drank and ate heartily.

When the British troops returned to their ships, much of Richmond was in ruins, and all that remained of a

Benedict Arnold was a brilliant but ambitious general under George Washington until 1779, when he betrayed the patriot cause in the hope of receiving more respect from the British.

A Two-Word Name for Traitor

Benedict Arnold is the most famous turncoat in American history. A brave officer for the American cause, he believed he was not being promoted as quickly as he deserved, and he defected to the British side, thinking he would be better appreciated by the British. After the war, he spent the rest of his life in England, but the British wanted nothing to do with a traitor—even one who betrayed his country for Britain.

nearby weapons factory were a furnace and chimney. The wooden warehouses that held the state's prized tobacco crops were also smoldering skeletons, as were many of the homes, most of them made of wood. Jefferson's enemies tried to blame him for not having protected the capital better. Even he doubted himself; he knew he was no military leader. Yet he also knew that if he had called the militia out two days earlier, they would still have been no match for the well-armed British.

The usually calm and reasonable Jefferson was enraged at Benedict Arnold. He wrote to his friend General J. P. G. Muhlenberg asking him to kill or capture the notorious traitor. For Jefferson, the war had become very personal.

A Heart Twice Broken

The spring brought more sorrow. Lucy Elizabeth, who had been born the previous fall, died in April. Jefferson took his sick and grieving wife and his daughters back home to Monticello to bury the baby. Then he moved the government to Charlottesville.

Jefferson was heartbroken by the condition of his beloved

state. Believing that others could better serve it during time of war, he wrote to the Assembly saying that he would not accept another term as governor when his term ended in June. Virginia needed a military leader, not a philosopher and statesman. He confessed that he was unprepared by his "line of life and education for the command of armies." He urged them to name as governor the head of the militia, General Thomas Nelson, Jr. The Assembly postponed choosing a new governor until June 4, two days after Jefferson's term officially ended. Little did they know that those two days would stretch to nearly two weeks.

On June 2, 1781, the last day of Jefferson's term, British Lieutenant-Colonel Banastre Tarleton and two hundred soldiers were riding toward Charlottesville to capture Jefferson, the Council of State, and the Virginia Assembly. The next night, when the troops stopped to rest at a tavern about forty miles from Charlottesville, Jack Jouett, a member of the militia, overheard their plans. He quietly slipped out the back door and rode through the night to warn Jefferson just as the sun was rising.

Jefferson quickly awakened his family and several Assembly

British Lieutenant-Colonel Tarleton nearly captured Governor Jefferson at Monticello in June 1781. Despite his reputation as a ruthless officer, Tarleton treated Jefferson's home and property with respect.

members who were staying with him. He calmly sent his wife and daughters off to safety at a neighboring farm. Having learned how destructive British troops could be, he also gave orders to his slaves about where to hide the family valuables.

He left Monticello through a back trail only five minutes before Tarleton and his men arrived. They stayed at Monticello for eighteen hours enjoying some of Jefferson's wine, but they touched little else. They had strict orders not to take or destroy anything.

The members of the Assembly scattered when they heard the news of the British arrival.

The members of the Assembly scattered when they heard the news of the British arrival. Some were captured, but a few days later forty members convened in Staunton, a town on the edge of Virginia's frontier, about two days' ride west. They waited another week before choosing Thomas Nelson as the new governor on June 12. Realizing that they had tied the governor's hands by limiting his authority, they gave Nelson powers that they had never granted Jefferson.

Virginia's humiliation was short lived. General George Washington had sent the Marquis de Lafayette, a French aristocrat who offered his services and money to the American Revolution, to command an army in Virginia. By late July 1781, Lafayette and fresh troops from the north had the British General Charles Cornwallis retreating across the state. Then, in October 1781, Lafayette trapped Cornwallis at Yorktown, on the Virginia coast. Surrounded on land and sea, the British surrendered and ended the war. America was free.

CHAPTER 5

Minister to France

I was much an enemy of monarchy before I came to Europe. Now I am ten thousand times more so since I have seen what they are.

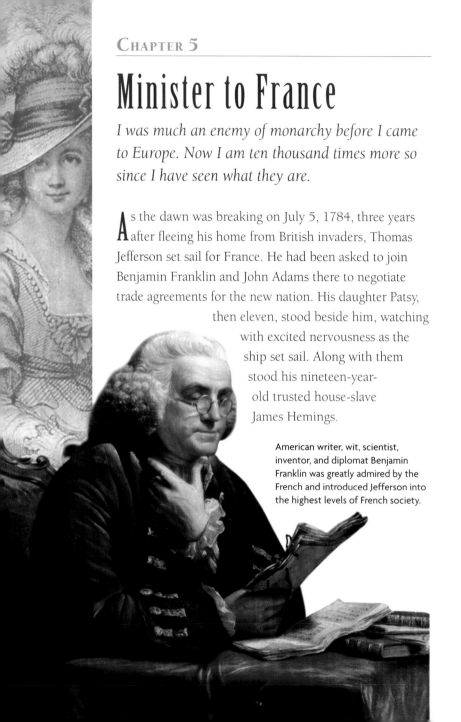

As the dawn was breaking on July 5, 1784, three years after fleeing his home from British invaders, Thomas Jefferson set sail for France. He had been asked to join Benjamin Franklin and John Adams there to negotiate trade agreements for the new nation. His daughter Patsy, then eleven, stood beside him, watching with excited nervousness as the ship set sail. Along with them stood his nineteen-year-old trusted house-slave James Hemings.

American writer, wit, scientist, inventor, and diplomat Benjamin Franklin was greatly admired by the French and introduced Jefferson into the highest levels of French society.

As his country shrank and disappeared from view, Jefferson thought of the life he was leaving behind. His beautiful wife had died nearly two years earlier, in September 1782, after giving birth to a little girl. The baby was named Lucy Elizabeth, for the daughter who had died a year earlier. Jefferson had been inconsolable after his wife died. For the following three weeks, he rarely left his room, and family and servants could hear him pacing back and forth anxiously.

As Patsy remembered it years later, "When at last he left his room he rode out and from that time he was incessantly on horseback…. In those melancholy rambles I was his constant companion, a solitary witness to many a violent burst of grief."

Then, in May 1784, when Congress asked Jefferson to join Franklin and Adams in Europe to negotiate trade agreements, he saw a chance for a new life. Jefferson had never crossed the ocean before. He was ready to work hard, and he was thrilled at the thought of feasting his eyes on the buildings, the art, and the gardens that he had been reading about since he was a boy.

Although he thought that Patsy was old enough to manage the grueling, dangerous trip to Europe, he decided that Polly and Lucy were better off staying in Virginia with Mrs. Jefferson's sister Elizabeth Eppes and her family. He knew that she would give his younger daughters the motherly love they both needed while he tended to the obligations of his country.

Jefferson's older daughter Martha, known to all as Patsy, posed for this portrait when she was an adult. She was devoted to her father throughout her life.

A Gray Winter

Paris was breathtaking. Every building, every street, every bridge seemed to have been built to please the eye. The gray, rainy weather, though, was a shock to Jefferson and Patsy. He suffered from colds and coughs for months—illness and the dreary weather made him homesick.

Within days of their arrival, Jefferson rode out to Benjamin Franklin's home. Franklin was then seventy-eight years old and ailing. Jefferson was very happy to see Franklin, who had kindly befriended his young colleague at the Continental Congress. The discoverer of electricity and author of *Poor Richard's Almanack*, Franklin was the first American celebrity in France.

While Franklin offered Jefferson a taste of French society, John and Abigail Adams offered him a very welcome taste of

Benjamin Franklin receives a laurel wreath from a member of the French court in this painting commemorating his presentation to King Louis XVI (seated, right) and Queen Marie Antoinette (seated, left).

America's First Superstar

When Benjamin Franklin arrived in 1776 as America's first minister to France, he was an instant celebrity. The surprised and delighted Franklin wrote to his daughter, "My picture is everywhere, on the lids of snuff boxes, on rings, busts. The numbers sold are incredible…. Your father's face is now as well known as the man in the moon."

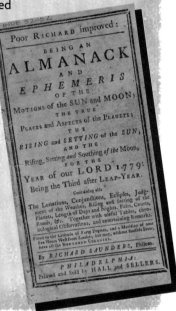

Benjamin Franklin's *Poor Richard's Almanac* was filled with witty sayings and wise advice such as "Early to bed and early to rise, makes a man healthy, wealthy, and wise."

home. Abigail took Patsy under her motherly wing. Their brilliant son, John Quincy, who in 1824 would himself be elected president, became like a son to Jefferson, spending as much time at Jefferson's home as he did at his own. Jefferson was happy to share his love of history with the intelligent and curious young man.

Jefferson, Franklin, and Adams worked hard together to craft agreements with European nations so that the United States could freely buy and sell goods there. It was a great responsibility. The states were depending on the three men. Without foreign trade, the new nation had no markets for its crops, fish, and game. The vengeful British had done a good job of convincing other European countries that the new nation was unstable and had little to offer. Jefferson and his two colleagues spent months writing agreements that few nations signed.

That first dreary winter brought tragic news from home. In January 1785, Jefferson learned that Polly, then six, and Lucy Elizabeth, then two, had come down with whooping cough, a severe infection that causes coughing fits and breathing trouble. Although Polly recovered, Lucy died. Jefferson was wracked with grief and guilt that he had not brought them with him to Paris. He desperately wanted Polly to join them, but he was afraid to risk her life in the dangerous sea crossing. He thought he would be back home with her before the end of the year, so he decided to let her remain in Virginia.

American Minister to France

By the middle of the year, though, Jefferson learned that his time in Paris would be longer than he expected. Franklin desperately wanted to return to Philadelphia, and Congress finally agreed to let him go; and Adams was heading to London to become America's first **ambassador** to England.

Hero of the American Revolution and friend of Jefferson, the Marquis de Lafayette introduced Jefferson to members of French society and helped him gain support for the new nation.

Jefferson was appointed to take Franklin's place as the **minister** to France.

Jefferson soon befriended a group of French nobles who acted as his guides to French society. The Marquis de Lafayette, whose aid to the patriots during the American Revolution helped turn the tide against the British, was glad to see Jefferson again. Jefferson also became a close friend of the Marquis de Chastellux, who had visited Monticello while the Frenchman led troops in Virginia during the war. Lafayette and Chastellux introduced Jefferson to important politicians and thinkers.

While in Paris, Jefferson fell in love with Maria Cosway, an Italian painter and wife of English portrait artist Richard Cosway. They remained friends throughout their lives.

Jefferson was astonished by the beauty of the furnishings and the breathtaking number of books available in Paris shops. He filled his house with thousands of new books and with elegant new furniture and household items, spending more than a year's salary on such objects and on clothes. By the time he left Paris, he had bought enough books to fill 250 feet of bookshelves.

Jefferson's contact with the French people was not limited to the wealthy. He was shocked by the poverty he saw in Paris and blamed the French king Louis XVI. "I was much an enemy of monarchy before I came to Europe. Now I am ten thousand times more so since I have seen what they are," he wrote to George Washington. The king "hunts one half the day, is drunk the other." Queen Marie Antoinette "is detested and an explosion of some sort is not impossible." The tensions between the rich and the poor that would lead to the French Revolution already concerned Jefferson.

But he was careful not to reveal his opinions publicly. He knew that the French court was reading his mail, and when he wrote letters to his friends about his real impressions, he always used secret codes.

Thomas Jefferson: Secret Agent

In February 1787, Jefferson told friends that for the next few months he would be traveling to the south of France to visit some baths that were famous for their healing power. Jefferson had fallen and broken his wrist several months earlier and it was not healing.

He journeyed with no servants, and hired carriage drivers

Secret Message Maker

To send secret messages, Jefferson invented a wheel cipher with twenty-six disks, each one with the alphabet printed in random order. He would click the disks in order to spell out a message across a row, and then copy out the random letters in the row above or below. The recipient would set the coded message on his identical cipher and read the real words in the row above or below.

This wheel cipher, invented by Jefferson, allowed messages to be scrambled by a sender and unscrambled by the receiver, who had an identical tool.

Jefferson admired the ancient Roman structures he saw in France. The Pont du Gard, built in 19 B.C., brought water over the Gardon River Valley to the city of Nimes.

and horses along the way. It was an odd way for a man to travel to a spa. But it was not so strange for a man who was on a secret mission: to learn more about European farms and ports in the hope of increasing American trade on the continent. He traveled alone because he thought he had a better chance of gathering information about crops and farming techniques than he would have as the American minister. Jefferson moved quietly through the countryside for three months, visiting small villages that many of his Parisian friends had never seen. His enthusiasm for everything he saw was boundless, and he did not limit himself to business pursuits. He went out of his way to see the ancient Roman ruins that he had studied since childhood. Their architectural beauty and engineering marvels fascinated him. Ever a curious and passionate farmer, he was also on the lookout

Thomas Jefferson sat for his first portrait in 1786 while minister to France. A statue of the goddess of Liberty stands behind him.

for new plants that could grow well in the South. He sent pistachio, almond, fig, and olive plants back home to establish new crops.

Jefferson returned from his trip a changed man. He had learned a great deal about European farming, seen many ancient ruins, and admired modern engineering feats. "I never passed three and a half months more delightedly," he told a friend.

Polly Comes to Paris

Shortly after Jefferson's return to Paris, his beloved daughter Polly finally joined him and Patsy. He had been arranging the journey for months. He wanted to make certain that she sailed only during the best weather and on a ship that was new enough to ensure her safety. Accompanying her was fourteen-year-old Sally Hemings, who was the sister of Jefferson's house-slave James. Sally had been Polly's trusted playmate for years. Polly had been only six when her father and sister left for France. Now she was nine. She hardly remembered them, but she soon adjusted to her new life. Although Polly was homesick at first, her charming disposition won over all who met her.

By autumn 1787, life for the Jeffersons settled into a familiar and comfortable routine. Outside their home, however, a dramatic crisis loomed. French society was collapsing. In France, the First and Second **Estates** were made up of

King Louis XVI of France is shown here in his coronation portrait in 1774. He ruled until 1792. He and his wife, Marie Antoinette, were beheaded the following year.

A crowd attacks the Bastille, a Paris prison, on July 14, 1789. Bastille Day is now a French national holiday, celebrating the beginning of the French Revolution.

priests and nobles who held great power and paid few taxes. The Third Estate was composed of peasants, who worked for food and shelter on farms in the country, and the bourgeoisie, which included merchants, manufacturers, bankers, doctors, lawyers, and intellectuals. The Third Estate paid all the taxes that supported the king's lavish lifestyle and the government. By 1789, driven by grinding poverty and skyrocketing prices, and inspired by the American Revolution, the peasants and the bourgeoisie had grown restless.

Poor people began rioting in July, but Jefferson remained confident that the wisdom of men like his friend Lafayette would guide the nation through a peaceful transition to **democracy**. Trying to remain officially neutral, Jefferson secretly helped Lafayette and others write a constitution for France in the summer of 1789.

In September, Jefferson, Patsy, and Polly, along with their servants James and Sally Hemings, packed up for a six-month visit home. It was time to find a husband for Patsy, who was then the marriageable age of seventeen, and Jefferson needed to tend to his farms. He thought he would return to Paris in the spring. But by the time they were boarding a ship for their return home in October, France was crumbling. Over the next ten years, France would be thrown into chaos as the king and queen were executed and a series of increasingly bloody governments took power.

While the family sailed across the ocean, their own lives were taking an unexpected turn. George Washington was writing to Jefferson to ask him to become the country's first secretary of state.

While the family sailed across the ocean, their own lives were taking an unexpected turn. George Washington was writing to Jefferson to ask him to become the country's first secretary of state. Due to the turmoil in France and because of the need to serve his government at home, Jefferson would never return to his beloved France again.

His five years in France were the happiest of his life. What he saw and learned there would transform him into one of the most worldly and sophisticated presidents in American history.

CHAPTER 6

The Reluctant Politician

[I am determined] to be liberated from the hated occupation of politics.

When Thomas Jefferson, Patsy, and Polly's ship sailed into port at Norfolk, Virginia, in November 1789, he heard the news that President George Washington had nominated him to be secretary of state. Jefferson was not sure what to think. He had returned to Virginia largely to find a suitable husband for Patsy. He had no intention of staying there more than a few months before returning to France.

As Jefferson was trying to decide whether to accept the nomination, he traveled home to Monticello. Along the way, he stopped in Richmond to see how construction was progressing on the new state capitol. He had designed the building while living in France, basing it on an ancient Roman temple that he had seen in Nimes. He hired a French architect who took Jefferson's rough drawings and rendered them so that builders could follow them, and he had a

George Washington as president. He convinced Jefferson to become his first secretary of state despite Jefferson's wish to return to France.

This plaster model, ordered by Jefferson, was based on an ancient Roman temple he had visited in France. It was used to construct the capitol in Richmond, Virginia.

plaster model of the building made and sent to Richmond. Jefferson was pleased with the progress. It would be "an edifice of first rate dignity" when it was finished, he said.

Duty Calls

On February 14, 1790, Jefferson chose patriotic duty over personal desire and accepted George Washington's nomination to become the nation's secretary of state. But before he did so, on February 23, 1790, Patsy was married to Thomas Mann Randolph, Jr. The groom was the son of Thomas Mann Randolph, an old friend and second cousin of Jefferson's, and the bride's father was delighted with the pairing.

After settling eleven-year-old Polly with her aunt, Jefferson set off on March 1 for New York, where the federal government was temporarily located. He quickly became lonely. "Having had yourself and dear Poll to live with me so long, to exercise my affections and cheer me in the intervals of business, I feel heavily the separation from you," he wrote to Patsy. Polly came to live

Gentleman-Farmer President

When George Washington resigned his commission as commander in chief in 1783 at the end of the Revolutionary War, he planned to spend the rest of his life happily farming his vast acres. But in 1789, he was unanimously chosen as America's first president. The reluctant gentleman farmer accepted his country's call and again sacrificed his personal life for the needs of his fledgling nation.

with him the following year, once he had settled in Philadelphia, the government's next temporary home.

Work soon left him little time for homesickness. As secretary of state, Jefferson was busy managing relationships with foreign countries. He was also responsible for domestic duties, including

Federal Hall in New York, where the first Federal Congress was held in 1789. The following year the capital moved to its second temporary home in Philadelphia.

publishing and distributing new laws and preserving all the records of the Continental Congress. These included the Constitution and the Declaration of Independence.

Washington's cabinet had only four members. In addition to Jefferson, there were Secretary of the Treasury Alexander Hamilton, who was responsible for financial matters; Secretary of War Henry Knox, who oversaw national defense; and Attorney General Edmund Randolph, who enforced the nation's laws and argued for the government before the **Supreme Court**. Not including the diplomats stationed in a handful of countries in Europe, Jefferson's entire staff at the State Department was made up of five people: two chief clerks, two assistant clerks, and a translator.

Jefferson versus Hamilton

As Jefferson was settling into his new job in the spring of 1790, Congress was deadlocked about how to pay for the costs of the American Revolutionary War. One day Hamilton asked Jefferson to use his influence on the southern members of Congress to reach a compromise on his debt-financing plan. Both men feared that squabbling over money could lead to the crumbling of the fragile new union.

Jefferson agreed to invite Hamilton, Virginia congressman James Madison

Alexander Hamilton, America's first secretary of the treasury, was opposed to Jefferson on almost every political issue. The two men's disputes became public as time wore on.

(Jefferson's friend and an opponent of the plan), and representatives from Maryland and Pennsylvania to his temporary home for dinner the next night to come up with something they could agree on. The plan worked. Two Maryland and two Virginia congressmen agreed to support the debt funding plan if the nation's permanent capital would be moved to the south—along the Potomac River.

Soon, though, Jefferson and Hamilton were working against each other, and their political disagreements became personal. The two men disagreed on every issue, from international relations to the formation of a national bank. Hamilton believed that a strong national government was key to the success of the new nation. Jefferson on the other hand held the view that the powers of the federal government should be limited, and he trusted in the wisdom of the citizens to make the right decisions. He feared that Hamilton's approach would align the government with powerful people and special interests at the expense of everyday citizens.

By the following year, their squabbles had become public. Using a pen name to hide his identity, Hamilton attacked Jefferson's policies in the *Gazette of the United States*, a national

Shaper of America's Finances

Alexander Hamilton, the first secretary of the treasury, was a passionate advocate of a strong central government. His public battles with Thomas Jefferson, who favored strong state governments and individual rights, have echoed through political generations to the present. Hamilton was killed by his political rival Aaron Burr, in a duel in 1804.

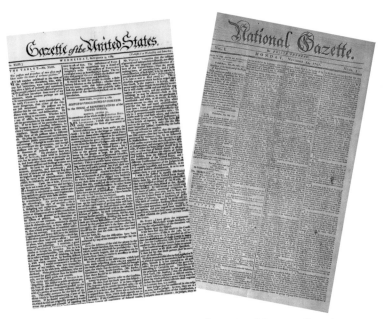

The *Gazette of the United States* represented Alexander Hamilton's Federalist philosophy of government. Using a pen name, Hamilton attacked Jefferson's policies and opinions—and at times his character.

The *National Gazette* reflected Jefferson's Republican political philosophy. Jefferson encouraged others, including his friend James Madison, to attack Hamilton and the Federalists at every turn.

paper representing Hamilton's perspective. He was answered in kind by anonymous articles written by Madison and others defending Jefferson in the *National Gazette*, a newspaper reflecting Jefferson's views. Although Jefferson never entered into the fray by writing articles, he urged others to do so and hired the editor of the *National Gazette*, Philip Freneau, as the State Department translator, giving him a steady income while he edited the newspaper.

Never one to relish a fight, Jefferson resigned from office on December 31, 1793, after nearly four years of bruising domestic and foreign policy battles. He told a friend that he was determined "to be liberated from the hated occupation of politics." He was happy to return to Monticello with fifteen-year-old Polly.

A Neglected Farm

Jefferson's ten-year absence serving his country in France and as secretary of state took a great toll on his farmlands. Although he had kept in contact with the farm's overseers while he was away, he was shocked at the condition of his estates when he returned. He quickly threw himself into revitalizing his land so that it could become profitable. He replenished the soil by planting different crops in each field during each new season. He also invented an improved moldboard plow for turning over the soil at planting time, and a compact horse-powered threshing machine to harvest wheat more efficiently.

Jefferson's plan for rotating crops in his fields to prevent the soil from becoming depleted was a radical idea. His planning helped improve the yield from his farms.

To supplement his income, and to pay for the construction on his mansion, he set up a nail-manufacturing shop at Monticello. A dozen teenage slaves worked there, supervised by Jefferson himself. Within a few years they were making a ton of nails a month.

"I am on horseback half the day, and counting and measuring nails the other half," he wrote to John Adams. But because he had difficulty finding buyers, the business was not as profitable as he had hoped. The local merchants bought their nails from suppliers who imported them—along with many other goods—from England. If they did not buy their nails from their suppliers, they risked losing other goods from them. Jefferson felt that he had been foiled by his old enemies, the British.

The Second Monticello

Many of the nails were used on the property at Monticello. When Jefferson returned there in January 1794, his beloved home was also showing signs of years of neglect. No matter. The elegant buildings and clever machines that improved daily life in France had inspired him to make dramatic changes to his home. The old Monticello had its fine points, but the Monticello he now had in mind was something else altogether.

The Salm mansion, built during Jefferson's time in Paris, inspired his renovation of Monticello.

Jefferson's study is seen here from his bedroom in Monticello. His built-in bed separates the two rooms.

His plans would transform it. His inspiration was Paris's Hôtel de Salm, a mansion that was built while he was living there. He had spent hours watching it while under construction and was, from the beginning, "violently smitten" with it.

He knocked down the old second story of Monticello and expanded the first floor to more than double its original size. The crowning achievement would be an octagonal dome room on the second floor above the original parlor. It was the first dome ever built over a house in America. The construction would take years to complete. In fact, Jefferson never really finished Monticello. Decades later, as an old man in retirement, he had plans for the estate that he could not have finished even if he had lived to be a hundred.

There was no house in America like Monticello. Jefferson filled it with furnishings that were unusual, if not unique. A

built-in bed separated his bedroom from his cabinet (or study). A revolving coat rack stood in an alcove at the foot of the bed. He could turn it with a long stick, allowing him to reach everything inside easily. And above the bed, accessible through a ladder, was built-in storage for out-of-season clothes.

Jefferson's study was filled with gadgets, including a machine that made a copy of each document he wrote, using a second pen that would "write" a copy as he wrote his original. He also designed a revolving bookstand that held five volumes open at a time. The other bedrooms had beds built into alcoves to save space and keep people warmer in the winter.

The great clock in Monticello's entrance hall was wound each week. The cannonball-like weights that made it run were hung on ropes extending through the floor into the basement.

On the outer wall of the entrance hall, he installed a two-faced clock: one facing the room, the other facing outside. A

With this copying machine called a polygraph, invented by John Isaac Hawkins, Jefferson made copies with a second pen as he wrote with the first.

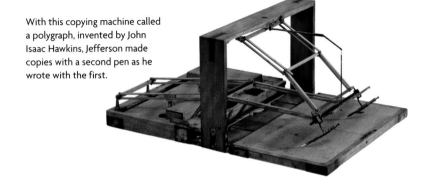

mallet struck a Chinese gong, which could be heard throughout the grounds, to announce the hours.

Politics Calls

Despite the demands on his time and attention of his farmland and house renovations, Jefferson soon began missing the political world that had dominated so much of his life. By 1796, as Washington's second term in office was ending, Jefferson was avidly reading newspapers again to keep track of the latest political wrangling.

When Washington announced that he would not seek a third term, the field was open for a replacement. John Adams, Washington's vice president, was a likely candidate, but his viewpoints were closer to Hamilton's than to Jefferson's. By this time political parties had begun to form. Those who believed in Hamiltonian ideas were called Federalists. Those who shared Jefferson's positions called themselves Republicans. When

Adams and Jefferson: Two Sides of the Same Coin

John Adams, the short, stout, and direct New Englander, and Thomas Jefferson, the tall, slender, and distant Virginian, made an odd couple. But beneath their differences lay a shared love of law and philosophy and a passionate belief in the new nation that they helped form.

Although political disputes separated them for a time, in their old age they reconnected and continued their passionate exchanges about philosophy, history, and the nation they loved.

Republicans looked around for a candidate with Jeffersonian ideals, they looked no further than Jefferson himself. From his mountaintop in Virginia, Jefferson did not discourage them from suggesting his name.

Neither Jefferson nor Adams campaigned during the election of 1796. They considered it beneath them. Rather than being elected by eligible citizens, presidents and vice presidents were chosen by the **Electoral College**. Each state chose their members for the Electoral College, either through popular elections or by vote of the state legislators, and the Electoral College voted for the candidates. When the votes were counted in 1796, Adams, with seventy-one electoral votes, defeated Jefferson by three votes. Other candidates included South Carolina congressman Thomas Pinckney and New York senator Aaron Burr.

In those days, the man with the second most votes became vice president. So Vice President–elect Jefferson headed once again to Philadelphia, the temporary seat of the federal government. He rode into the city just before the inauguration, hoping to slip into town quietly. But he was greeted by a crowd of supporters shooting guns in the air, cheering, and raising a banner saying "Jefferson the Friend of the People." He was pleased to be back among them.

Controversy seemed to follow Aaron Burr. A senator and Jefferson's first vice president, he killed his rival Alexander Hamilton in a duel and was later arrested for treason.

CHAPTER 7

An "Honorable and Easy" Office

I am for free commerce with all nations; political connections with none.

When John Adams and Thomas Jefferson took the oaths of office as president and vice president on March 4, 1797, the old friends met in a spirit of cooperation and goodwill. Jefferson was content with his position. The "second office is honorable and easy," he wrote. "The first is but splendid misery."

But the collaboration did not last long. Jefferson was surprised when, within days, Adams had made it clear that the vice president would not be involved in any policy matters. Partisan politics was taking charge, and the Republican Jefferson's role would be only to act as president of the **Senate**. All of Adams's advisers were Federalists who had served under Washington.

The XYZ Affair

Had Jefferson been more involved in policy making, America might have avoided a diplomatic conflict that took the country to the brink of war. France believed that an earlier treaty signed by the U.S. had favored Britain, so in the spring of 1797, France protested by rejecting Charles Cotesworth Pinckney as the new American

Scientist Jefferson

On the evening before Jefferson's inauguration as vice president, he was elected to an office that brought him great delight. He was chosen president of the American Philosophical Society, the nation's most important scientific organization at that time. Jefferson would remain its president until 1815.

A week after becoming president of the society, Jefferson presented a paper about the bones of a prehistoric creature that had been found in western Virginia by John Stuart, a former scout and Indian fighter. Jefferson named the creature Megalonyx, which means "great claw." The creature was later named *Megalonyx jeffersonii*, in honor of Jefferson. It was a huge, ox-sized ground sloth that had wandered through North America during the Ice Age.

Jefferson presented a paper in 1797 about the Megalonyx (or "great claw"), a giant prehistoric ground sloth. It marked the birth of paleontology, the study of fossils, in America.

Jefferson's fascination with the rich history of the animals that once lived in North America would continue throughout his life. He supported scientific research and exchanged lively letters with scientists throughout the world about their latest discoveries. His friends and colleagues at the society provided him with a community of like minds in Philadelphia, where he was an outsider in the Adams administration.

Jefferson always carried tabbed ivory note cards and a pencil with him. He could record information, copy it into notebooks at home, and erase the cards to reuse.

minister. Adams was outraged when he learned of France's action, and he called a special session of Congress, where he accused the French of treating the young nation "neither as allies or friends nor as a sovereign state." Jefferson, who believed in quiet diplomacy and loved the French, was shocked by Adams's tone and the anti-French talk among the Federalists.

In the summer of 1797, President Adams dispatched three representatives to the French government to try to mend fences. The American government waited nervously for word from Paris.

In March 1798, Secretary of State Timothy Pickering received coded messages from the representatives, saying that agents of the French government (codenamed X, Y, and Z) demanded that President Adams apologize for his speech to Congress, that the Americans loan the French government a large amount of money, and that America pay the three agents a $50,000 bribe before negotiations with the French foreign minister could begin.

Adams was incensed by the French demands, and when Congress published the XYZ papers, anti-French sentiment swept throughout the country. Jefferson, who knew the French very well,

Charles Cotesworth Pinckney, here in his South Carolina militia uniform, was rejected by France when he was appointed minister by John Adams. The resulting uproar nearly caused a war.

thought Adams was overreacting. He was convinced that the Americans had been swindled by the agents—probably without any knowledge of the leaders of the French government. He also believed that the French would become cooperative again if Adams would simply apologize for his remarks.

The Alien Act of 1798 permitted the detention or expulsion of non-citizens who were pro-France. The act was passed in response to rising tensions between the two nations.

Alien and Sedition Acts

But the time for apologies seemed to have passed. And the threat of war brought several new acts by Congress that concerned Jefferson even more than the idea of war itself. In the summer of 1798, Congress passed the Alien and **Sedition** Acts, which dramatically limited individual rights. The first alien act temporarily gave the president the right to deport any alien (noncitizen) that he believed to be "dangerous to the peace and safety of the United States." The act was applicable only during the crisis with France. The second alien act gave the president the permanent right to imprison or deport citizens of an enemy nation during times of war.

More alarming to Jefferson was the Sedition Act, which made it unlawful to write, say, or publish "any false, scandalous and malicious writing" against the president or Congress. Jefferson saw this act as an attempt to silence criticism by Republican politicians and journalists. The act was, he believed, an attack on the hard-won freedoms of speech and **assembly** spelled out in the Bill of Rights to the Constitution.

The tensions between France and the U.S. would continue for several years. French ships raided American merchant ships and America strengthened its army and navy, but neither side declared war. Finally, in 1799, President Adams sent a new delegation to France to negotiate a treaty. An agreement was signed in 1800, ending the hostilities and reestablishing trade between the two nations. The atmosphere of impending war and the assault on civil liberties, though, cast a shadow over Adams's administration and the election of 1800.

The Election of 1800

The beliefs held by Adams and the Federalists were in direct opposition to Jefferson's. To fight them, Jefferson took a bold but secretive stance in the summer of 1797, becoming the leader of the Republicans. Jefferson's strategic thinking and behind-the-scenes planning with state leaders would prove masterful in strengthening his party.

Jefferson defined the issues on which the Republicans would run in the coming federal and state elections. These included preserving the Constitution, protecting the Bill of Rights from being weakened, and limiting the rights of the federal government. He opposed a standing army during peacetime and wanted a navy strong enough only to protect American ports. Finally, he wanted America to avoid wars with Europe. "I am for free commerce with all nations; political connections with none," Jefferson wrote.

The lines were clearly drawn. A leading Republican newspaper, the Philadelphia *Aurora*, cut right to the chase: "The friends of peace will vote for Jefferson—the friends of war will vote for Adams…," wrote *Aurora* editor Benjamin Franklin Bache. In Republican newspapers George Washington was called a liar who longed to be a dictator and Adams was painted as a warmonger who had won office in 1796 by trickery.

The lines were clearly drawn. The leading Republican newspaper, the Philadelphia Aurora, cut right to the chase: "The friends of peace will vote for Jefferson—the friends of war will vote for Adams…"

The attacks on both sides were vicious. Jefferson was accused of being a lover of France who would lead America to war with Britain. His religious views were also attacked, and he was accused of being immoral. One minister preached that to vote for Jefferson was "no less than a rebellion against God." But the assaults on Jefferson's religion may have actually helped his campaign. His defense of religious freedom and his attacks on state religion had earned him admirers among the many Protestant sects that were growing throughout the country.

Another force was involved in the election of 1800. More people were allowed to vote. Voting rights previously had been limited to men who owned a certain amount of land. But as the 1790s progressed, states loosened their property requirements for voting. The hardworking poor and the self-made middle class, who now could vote for state representatives and the electors, saw the Federalists as elitists. Although Jefferson himself was born to wealth, his ideals better reflected those of everyday working people.

Furthermore, the number of electors was determined by the population of each state, and each slave was counted as three-fifths of a person. This gave southern states a distinct advantage in the election by increasing their number of representatives without giving slaves any voting rights.

The Votes Are Counted

By the time the electoral votes were counted in 1800, Thomas Jefferson and fellow Republican Aaron Burr, who had been nominated as vice president, were tied with seventy-three votes each; John Adams had sixty-five votes; Federalist vice presidential nominee Charles Cotesworth Pinckney received sixty-four votes; and New York governor John Jay got one vote.

The Republicans had won, but the question now was who would become president? The ambitious Burr refused to give one of his electoral votes to Jefferson to solve the problem. In case of a tie, the Constitution gave the final vote to the **House of Representatives**. A new president was to be elected by the Federalist-controlled House. Each state was given one vote. The House went through thirty-three ballots, all of them resulting in a tie between Jefferson and Burr.

Political Puzzle

Aaron Burr, Jefferson's first vice president, ended his career under a dark cloud of controversy. He killed his political rival Alexander Hamilton in a duel in 1804. Then, in 1807, Burr was tried for treason for a plan to establish a new nation in Mexican territory and encourage western states to secede. Acquitted of the charges, he fled to Europe. Four years later, he returned to New York and practiced law.

Alexander Hamilton and Aaron Burr meet in a duel. Burr challenged Hamilton for spreading damaging information about him in an election. Hamilton was killed and Burr was charged with murder.

Finally, several Federalist-controlled states that had been voting for Burr decided not to cast a vote for either candidate, submitting instead blank pieces of paper into the ballot box. No Federalist Congressman could bear to cast a vote for Jefferson, but by submitting blank votes, they broke the tie, and Jefferson became president without any Federalist votes.

The Second Revolution

Despite the wrangling and ill will, the election of 1800 was the first time in America that power was transferred from one political party to another. Looking back, Jefferson later called the election "as real a revolution in the principles of our government as that of 1776 was in its form." He had masterminded that revolution without spilling a drop of blood.

But the victory came with a price. John Adams, Jefferson's old friend who years before helped him write the Declaration of Independence and worked with him to establish America's ties in Europe, slipped out of the capital before dawn on inauguration day rather than witness Jefferson take the oath of office. After the bitter campaign, the two men did not speak again for twelve years.

Thomas Jefferson's place in history is carved in granite in Mount Rushmore. George Washington, Jefferson, Theodore Roosevelt, and Abraham Lincoln represent, respectively, America's independence, democratic process, world leadership, and equality.

CHAPTER 8

A Triumphant President

It keeps me from 10 to 12 to 13 hours a day at my writing table.

On the brisk, clear morning of March 4, 1801, Thomas Jefferson stepped out the door of Conrad and McMunn's boardinghouse in Washington, D.C., ready to become the first president to be inaugurated in the nation's new capital city. Accompanied by officers of the Alexandria, Virginia, militia; the secretaries of the navy and the treasury; and a few other political friends, Jefferson walked several muddy blocks to the still-unfinished Capitol building, where the ceremony would take place. The Senate Chamber, the only finished room in the building, was filled with members of the Senate and the House of Representatives and guests. John Marshall, the chief justice of the Supreme Court, swore in the new president.

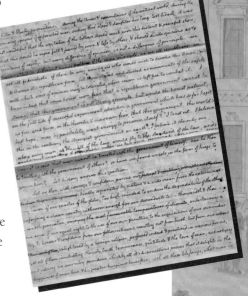

A page from Jefferson's draft of his first inaugural address. Seeking to heal wounds from the bitter election, he said, "We are all republicans: we are all federalists."

A few weeks after the inauguration, Jefferson moved into the President's House, as the White House was then called. He was the second president to live there. John and Abigail Adams had moved in during the last months of Adams's administration.

Still under construction, the place was a mess. As a man whose own house had been under constant alteration, the disarray did not bother Jefferson, but the shoddy workmanship did. The leaking roof was damaging ceilings and furniture. He quickly began overseeing the work and making design decisions, including having the heavy slate tiles removed from the buckling

The north wing of the U.S. Capitol, where President Jefferson was inaugurated in 1801. He walked there from his boardinghouse along muddy roads lined with cheering citizens.

A Frustrated Architect

Using a pseudonym to hide his identity, Thomas Jefferson is believed to have submitted an entry in the competition to design the President's House. He lost the contest. The President's House, now known as the White House, was designed by James Hoban, an Irish-born architect. Jefferson was not impressed with the building when he moved in. The roof leaked terribly, and the grounds were filled with trash left by workmen.

This ad offered a $500 prize and a medal for the winning design of the President's House, as the White House was then known.

WASHINGTON, in the Territory of COLUMBIA.

A PREMIUM

OF FIVE HUNDRED DOLLARS, or a MEDAL of that value, at the option of the party, will be given by the Commissioners of the Federal Buildings, to the person who, before the fifteenth day of July next, shall produce to them the most approved PLAN, if adopted by them, for a PRESIDENT's HOUSE, to be erected in this City. The fize of the building, if the artist will attend to it, will of courfe influence the afpect and outline of his plan; and it's deftination will point out to him the number, fize, and diftribution of the apartments. It will be a recommendation of any plan, if the central part of it may be detached and erected for the prefent, with the appearance of a complete whole, and be capable of admitting the additional parts, in future, if they fhall be wanting. Drawings will be expected of the ground plats, elevations of each front, and fections through the building, in fuch directions as may be necessary to explain the internal ftructure; and an eftimate of the cubic feet of brick-work compofing the whole mafs of the walls. THE COMMISSIONERS.

March 14, 1792. tf

roof and replacing them with lighter sheet metal. He even ordered the construction of low pavilions, or wings, on the east and west sides, to create more office space and improve the beauty of the building.

A Typical Day for President Jefferson

The focus of Jefferson's days was not on architecture, though. He worked long hours shaping the country's policy. "It keeps me from 10 to 12 to 13 hours a day at my writing table, giving me an interval of 4 hours for riding, dining, and a little unbending." He rose at five each morning and sat down at his desk early, reading reports from his cabinet members and doing other paperwork. At nine o'clock he would meet informally with cabinet members or members of Congress who came to see him. Appointments were not necessary.

Some people were taken aback by Jefferson's informal style. William Plumer, a newly elected Federalist senator who came to meet the president, was surprised by what he saw as he waited in a reception room. "In a few minutes, a tall high-boned man came into the room. He was dressed in an old brown coat, a red waistcoat, much soiled, woolen hose, and slippers without heels." The senator thought the man was a servant. He

This shabby red under waistcoat is believed to have been worn often by Jefferson. He had an extra lining sewn in to protect him from the cold.

was shocked when a colleague introduced him to the president. Once Plumer got over his surprise, Jefferson charmed him. "He is easy of access, and conversed with great ease and freedom," Plumer told a friend.

Jefferson did take some time for enjoyment each day. After a one-hour cabinet meeting at noon, Jefferson would have his horse Wildair saddled up for a ride around Washington. People would often spot Jefferson, dressed in his riding overalls, exploring the city and the surrounding area along the Potomac River. He would frequently stop to examine unfamiliar plants or rock formations, often bringing plant samples back to the President's House for further study.

Jefferson had his dinner at three thirty each afternoon. Three times a week he would invite a dozen or so guests—sometimes Federalists, sometimes Republicans—to dine with him around an oval table. People sat wherever they pleased. He did dress for the occasion, however. When Senator Plumer was invited to dinner, he happily reported that the president was wearing "a new suit of black, silk hose, shoes, [and] clean linen, and his hair [was] highly powdered," as was the fashion of the day.

The conversation was lively. Whether discussing the latest laws being considered, or a new treatment for waterproofing fabric, Jefferson seemed knowledgeable and curious about everything. At these dinner parties he established close personal relationships with members of Congress and his own administration. Often, by the time dessert was served, he had managed to persuade many people to agree with him on whatever issue was being discussed.

Often, by the time dessert was served, he had managed to persuade many people to agree with him on whatever issue was being discussed.

Jefferson expected his dinner guests to be gone by six o'clock. He still had an evening's worth of work to do. He would continue writing and reading at his desk until ten each evening, taking care of government business, sending letters to friends, and keeping up on the latest scientific discoveries. Occasionally he would attend a play or music concert.

In his study, his only companion was his pet mockingbird, Dick. Dick would serenade the president, and when no one else was there, Jefferson would open the bird's cage so he could fly around. The bird often sat on Jefferson's shoulder while the president worked, and would gently take food that Jefferson placed between his lips. Jefferson spent much of his time in Washington without his family. Although both of his daughters would act as hostesses for him from time to time, Patsy and her husband managed Monticello in his absence and were adding to their growing family. Eventually they would have twelve children. Polly had married John Wayles Eppes, her cousin, at Monticello while Jefferson was vice president, and they lived on their farm near the mansion. Jefferson regularly wrote loving letters to them both.

The Louisiana Purchase

Within weeks of becoming president, Jefferson received word from Europe that Spain was secretly negotiating a peace treaty that would turn over the vast Spanish-controlled Louisiana territory to France. The U.S. and Spain had cooperated on the use of New Orleans as a port for the settlers living along the Mississippi, and Spain was too weak to threaten America's western expansion. Jefferson worried that if France, a much stronger power, took possession of Louisiana, "we must marry ourselves to the British fleet and nation" for protection, a fate he wished to avoid at all costs. He ordered his agents in Spain and France to discourage the deal, but he kept the developments secret from

Thomas Jefferson's most faithful companion during his White House years was Dick, a mockingbird. These talented songbirds have been known to have up to forty different "tunes" in their repertoire.

The Louisiana Purchase of 1803 made Jefferson a national hero and more than doubled the size of the United States.

Congress members until later, when he thought they needed to be informed.

By then 20 percent of America's population was living along the Mississippi, and getting crops, hides, and raw materials to market was critical to survival on the frontier. "The Mississippi is to them everything," Jefferson wrote to the U.S. ambassador to Spain, "the Hudson, the Delaware, the Potomac, and all the navigable rivers of the Atlantic States formed into one stream."

In the meantime, Jefferson's envoy to Paris, Robert Livingston,

The Louisiana Purchase treaty was deliberately vague. Several more years of negotiations and treaties were needed to settle final boundaries.

In this cartoon against the Louisiana Purchase, Jefferson, a scrawny dog, is stung by a Napoleon hornet and coughs up "Two Millions" before a dancing Frenchman.

had received hints that France might be willing to negotiate with the U.S. for parts of Louisiana once Spain turned it over to French control. Then, on April 11, 1803, in Paris, the French foreign minister asked the shocked Livingston if America would be interested in buying all of Louisiana. Livingston could not believe his ears.

Napoleon Bonaparte, the general who had become the leader of France, had overextended his troops as he tried to conquer Europe. He was planning another war with Britain and feared that the Louisiana territory would be vulnerable to

The military skill of France's Napoleon Bonaparte is saluted in this painting. He needed money to conquer Europe, so he sold the Louisiana territory to the U.S.

British attack. He preferred to use the funds from the sale to finance his war rather than potentially lose the land to Britain at a great cost. By the end of the month, an agreement was reached to sell the land to America for $15 million. The estimated area was 909,130 square miles, which came out to about $16.50 per square mile.

The Louisiana Purchase more than doubled the size of the United States and included the area making up the modern states of Louisiana, Arkansas, Missouri, Iowa, Minnesota, Nebraska, Oklahoma, Kansas, most of North Dakota and South Dakota, and parts of New Mexico, Texas, Montana, Wyoming, and Colorado.

The Lewis and Clark Expedition

Jefferson hungered for the land that stretched in the northwest all the way to the Rocky Mountains. He told Congress that the purchase would help trade. On a personal level, he was intrigued by the promise of scientific discoveries of unimaginable plants and animals in the west. Several years before, when the land still belonged to Spain, Jefferson had asked permission to explore the region. His request had been denied, but Jefferson had quietly gone ahead with plans to send a small team out there.

Meriwether Lewis, a twenty-six-year-old Monticello neighbor,

Jefferson chose Meriwether Lewis, a neighbor and friend, to lead his expedition to the western territories. "I could have no hesitation in confiding the enterprise to him."

Corps of Discovery

Thomas Jefferson's dream of exploring the West was realized in May 1804, when Meriwether Lewis and William Clark led a group of thirty-one men and Seaman, a "dogg of the newfoundland breed," from St. Louis, Missouri, up the Missouri River. The thirty-three members of the Corps of Discovery were trained in botany, wilderness survival, medicine, and Indian languages, and their two-year journey became the stuff of legend.

They spent the winter of 1804–05 camped near the Mandan Sioux in what is present-day North Dakota. There they hired a French trader, Toussaint Charbonneau, and his Shoshone Indian wife, Sacagawea, to translate for them when they headed west in the spring. That winter, Sacagawea gave birth to a son, whom she

Lewis and Clark's Corps of Discovery on the upper Columbia River. Their journey, painted by C. M. Russell, captured the nation's imagination.

carried on her back throughout the expedition. Her knowledge of edible plants helped supplement their diets, and her bravery and strength were extraordinary. Having a woman and baby on the expedition, they soon discovered, was "a token of peace," as Clark wrote in his journal, and the group was welcomed by other Indian peoples during their journey to the Pacific.

The explorers encountered grizzly bears, rattlesnakes, hostile Indians, and treacherous conditions on their journey to the west coast. The animal specimens they sent back and their sketches and journal descriptions of the plants, animals, and natural formations that they saw contributed greatly to scientific knowledge and to a national fascination with the West.

Sacagawea, a Shoshone translator, guides the Lewis and Clark explorers across the Rocky Mountains in this twentieth-century painting.

was a captain in the army of the West who knew several Indian languages when Jefferson asked him to become his secretary in 1801. Jefferson did not need a man to write letters for him, since he wrote his own letters and speeches. Jefferson's real reason for choosing Lewis was so that, when the time was right, Jefferson could send him out to explore the West. To prepare for the journey, Lewis spent more than a year in Philadelphia studying botany, zoology, and basic medicine at the University of Pennsylvania.

William Clark shared command of the Corps of Discovery. A talented artist, he mapped the journey and sketched the wildlife they encountered.

In early 1803, even before Jefferson had received word that France was offering to sell him the region, he secretly got Congress to pay for an expedition "for the purpose of extending the external commerce of the U.S." More important to Jefferson, the explorers were to study the land, plants, and animals as carefully as possible. It was, in fact, to be the first scientific expedition supported by the government. He asked Lewis to lead the Corps of Discovery, as the team was called.

More important to Jefferson, the explorers were to study the land, plants, and animals as carefully as possible.

Lewis invited fellow Virginian William Clark to lead the group with him. Lewis had served under Clark in the army of the

West and trusted his ability and judgment. In June 1803, Jefferson gave Lewis detailed instructions for the mission, and Lewis set off from Washington for St. Louis, where the team and their supplies would be assembled. By the time they left St. Louis the following year, the expedition also had a political purpose. Lewis and Clark had to explain to the Indian tribes and any traders they encountered along the way that the land once owned by Spain and France was now part of the United States. Two agonizing years would pass before Jefferson would receive his first report from Lewis and Clark about their dangerous mission.

Although 1804 was a year of political triumph for Jefferson, it was also a year of personal tragedy.

With widespread support for the Louisiana Purchase, which officially passed into American hands in December 1803, Jefferson was swept back into office in 1804. Despite another nasty campaign filled with personal attacks on Jefferson, he received 162 electoral votes against 14 for Charles Cotesworth Pinckney, his Federalist opponent.

Although 1804 was a year of political triumph for Jefferson, it was also a year of personal tragedy. In April, his daughter Polly, at the age of twenty-five, died following the birth of her daughter Maria. Jefferson was shattered to lose one of his only two surviving children. "Others may lose of their abundance but I, of my own want, have lost even the half of all I had," he wrote to his old friend John Page. Nearly a year later, Jefferson was still in mourning. On his inauguration in March 1805, he was dressed in black as he rode to the Capitol to take the oath of office.

CHAPTER 9

A Nation Under Siege

What an awful spectacle does the world exhibit at this instant.

Thomas Jefferson delivered his second inaugural address in March 1805 "in so low a voice that not half of it was heard by any part of the crowded auditory," remembered Senator John Quincy Adams, the son of former president John Adams. In it, Jefferson looked back over the previous four years proudly. In his first administration, Jefferson had been able to take advantage of the constant tensions in Europe, buying Louisiana at a fire-sale price, and bringing a wealth of goods and money into American hands through trading with the warring nations. By the end of his second term, though, those European conflicts that had benefited Americans would shift, and the country's newfound wealth would evaporate.

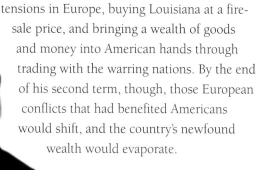

John Quincy Adams, son of John Adams, spent a life in devoted service to his country as congressman, senator, diplomat, and president.

Tensions Mount in Europe

The language in the treaty for the Louisiana Purchase was vague about what were the borders with Spanish-controlled Florida. Jefferson was determined to acquire West Florida (the coastal regions of present-day Alabama and Mississippi). Spain, though, was still smarting from France's quick sale of the region that it had won from Spain in 1800. Spain was in no mood to give up more territory. Jefferson had sent James Monroe to Europe to settle the boundaries between Louisiana and Florida, but Spain refused to negotiate with him. As tensions mounted, Jefferson considered simply seizing all of Florida from Spain. He wanted to make sure that Europe would have no control over any part of North America.

America turned to France in the hope that it would convince Spain to settle the borders, but France was unwilling to help. General John Armstrong, whom Jefferson sent to Paris to ask the French to persuade Spain, quickly realized that France was encouraging the tensions between them. France, he said, saw Spain and the United States as "a couple of oranges in her hands which she will squeeze at pleasure, and against each other, and that which yields the most will be the best served or rather the least injured."

In 1805, France was extending its empire on land, taking control of much of Europe, while Britain was becoming master of the seas. "What an awful spectacle does the world exhibit at this instant," Jefferson complained in January 1806, "one man bestriding the continent of Europe like a Colossus and another

> *In 1805, France was extending its empire on land, taking control of much of Europe, while Britain was becoming master of the seas.*

roaming unbridled on the ocean." As the relationship between France and Britain deteriorated, navigating peacefully between them grew more difficult. Each delivery of letters seemed to bring more disappointing news from Europe. The news from the West, however, was far more encouraging.

Lewis and Clark Return

Jefferson's second administration had few joyful moments, but one came in October 1806, when Jefferson learned that the expedition led by Meriwether Lewis and William Clark had returned safely to St. Louis, more than two years after leaving to explore the lands acquired in the Louisiana Purchase.

The first scientific expedition in America was a great success. The explorers traveled all the way to the Pacific Ocean, reaching the mouth of the Columbia River in present-day Oregon.

Lewis and Clark's journey from St. Louis, Missouri, to Fort Clatsop, Oregon, and back covered more than seven thousand miles and opened a world of possibility to the new nation.

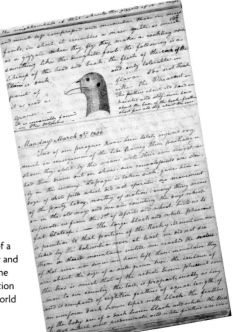

William Clark's sketch of a sage grouse. His artistry and detailed notes during the Lewis and Clark Expedition brought to life a new world of natural history to America.

Jefferson was thrilled with Lewis and Clark's detailed accounts of their journey, which included descriptions, drawings, and samples of plants and animals never before seen by American scientists.

Lewis and Clark also sent back several live examples of some unusual animals they found on their journey, including a magpie and a prairie dog, which Jefferson sent to Charles Willson Peale, a fellow member of the American Philosophical Society, for his museum in Philadelphia.

Challenged at Sea

Jefferson's political challenges dealing with Europe seemed at least as death defying as Lewis and Clark's physical challenges. His old feelings toward Britain had not changed much since the

Revolution. He still did not trust the British. But his once fond feelings toward France had changed. He was very wary of their hunger for an empire.

The British enforced an **embargo** against French trade with its Caribbean colonies, an important source of food for Napoleon's armies. Until 1805, Britain allowed American merchants to trade with France and its Caribbean colonies

HMS *Victory*, the flagship of Admiral Horatio Nelson, British naval commander during the American Revolution and the Napoleonic Wars, helped establish Britain's control over the world's seas.

through a loophole called "reimportation." Under this practice, American traders had been importing goods from French colonies in the West Indies, bringing them to the U.S. briefly, and then exporting them to France, going around the British embargo against the French—and making a tidy profit. When the British declared reimportation illegal in 1805, British ships seized nearly four hundred American merchant ships, crippling American trade.

Around the same time, British warships also began boarding American merchant ships looking for British sailors who had deserted their military ships. Desertion was a big problem for the British navy. The conditions on British naval ships were terrible, and the risk of death during a battle was very high. Desperate sailors would abandon ship in American ports and sign on to American trading vessels, where the conditions and pay were better. About one quarter of the men sailing on American merchant ships were former British sailors. Traders from the southern states particularly relied on British crewmen.

The conditions on British naval ships were terrible, and the risk of death during a battle was very high.

Although the British regularly boarded merchant ships, they agreed, on principle, not to board military ships. Then, in June 1807, the U.S. navy warship *Chesapeake*, manned by a large number of British deserters, set out from Norfolk, Virginia, for

USS Chesapeake

After four men were seized by the HMS *Leopard* from the USS *Chesapeake* for desertion from the British navy, the *Chesapeake* saw more dramatic action. During the **War of 1812**, it squared off against the HMS *Shannon* in the war's bloodiest naval battle. The *Chesapeake* was confiscated by the British navy and sailed under the British flag until the end of the War of 1812.

When the USS *Chesapeake* was seized by the HMS *Shannon* during the War of 1812, its commander's dying words were "don't give up the ship," which became a navy motto.

duty in the Mediterranean. Some of the deserters had brazenly insulted British officers while they were on shore in Norfolk, and the officers were furious.

Shortly after the *Chesapeake* left port, a British warship, the HMS *Leopard*, approached and demanded that the deserters be turned over. When American Commodore James Barron refused, the *Leopard* fired at the ship, killing three men and wounding eighteen, including Barron. Then British sailors boarded the *Chesapeake* and removed four crewmen whom they claimed were deserters.

When the *Chesapeake* returned to Norfolk, news of the incident spread throughout the country. The American public seemed hungry for war with Britain. Throughout the summer, Jefferson waited anxiously in Washington and then at Monticello for word from Halifax, where the men were to be tried for desertion, and from London, where Monroe and Pinckney tried to negotiate a settlement.

Up to that point, Jefferson had managed to remain neutral in the French and British conflict. But during his summer vacation at Monticello, he learned that the four men seized from the *Chesapeake* had been court-martialed, and one of them had been hanged. Jefferson concluded that war with Britain was inevitable. "I never expected to be under the necessity of wishing success to Bonaparte.... I cannot, with Anglomen, prefer a certain present evil to a future hypothetical one."

And if war were to come, he would use it as an excuse to spring on the Spanish in Florida, seizing the entire colony for America by force. Although his immediate problems were

James Madison, Jefferson's friend and confidant, became the fourth president of the United States. Madison's political skills helped make Jefferson's vision a reality.

Jefferson's "Pillar of Support"

James Madison was Thomas Jefferson's closest friend and political ally. Their friendship stretched from their days in the Virginia Assembly in 1776 until Jefferson's death. Madison, a shrewd politician, led the Republicans and created alliances to support Jefferson's vision. They spent so much time discussing history and politics together that one guest bedroom in Monticello was known as "Mr. Madison's room."

with Europe, his vision for the future was to create an "Empire of Liberty" in North America, stretching from the Atlantic to the Pacific.

Embargo

As the summer faded into fall, the American public, which had a short memory, had lost its taste for battle with Britain over the *Chesapeake* affair. When Congress met in October, Jefferson realized that public opinion had changed. The House and the Senate decided not to declare war against Britain.

Later that year, though, tensions over British soldiers jumping ship to join the American fleet rose again. In December, Congress passed an embargo against Britain. Secretary of State James Madison, a strong supporter of the embargo, believed that it would deprive Britain of the basic goods it needed to feed and clothe its people. Soon, he thought, the British would back down, apologize, and stop boarding American ships in search of wayward sailors.

The embargo was a disaster. For the British, it was a mere

inconvenience, but for the Americans it was economically crippling. Americans suddenly had no markets to sell their goods. Soon, resourceful traders were using overland routes to take their goods through Canada to market in Britain. Enforcing the embargo became a nightmare that lasted throughout Jefferson's final year in office. The headaches that had plagued him throughout his life when he was under stress were especially severe at this time. One particularly bad episode kept him in his darkened room for three weeks.

The embargo was a disaster. For the British, it was a mere inconvenience, but for the Americans it was economically crippling. Americans suddenly had no markets to sell their goods.

He found it hard to believe that citizens would so brazenly defy the law. "This embargo law is certainly the most embarrassing one we have ever had to execute," he wrote. "I did not expect a crop of so sudden and rank growth of fraud and open opposition by force could have grown up in the U.S." His belief in his fellow Americans was shaken.

Shaking Off the Shackles of Power

Jefferson's final year in office was agonizing. More than a year before his term ended, he confessed to Monroe, "My longings for retirement are so strong that I with difficulty encounter the daily drudgeries of my duty."

In 1808, Jefferson seemed to stop being the confident leader he had been throughout the seven previous years. Congress, which looked to him for guidance, was unable to decide whether to continue the unpopular embargo, wage war with Britain, or simply give up. During his final months in office, he left major policy-making decisions to the next president.

"On this occasion, I think it is fair to leave to those who are to act on them, the decisions they prefer, being to be myself but a spectator," he said in November 1808, as electoral ballots were being gathered and counted for his successor. Still four months from the end of his term, he seemed to have lost interest in politics. James Madison, who would become president, would have to make those difficult decisions. Jefferson was more than ready to retire to Monticello.

During the inauguration, one of the guests said, "Mr. Jefferson appeared one of the most happy among this concourse of people."

On March 4, 1809, Jefferson attended the inauguration of his old friend. Shortly before that day, he wrote, "Never did a prisoner, released from his chains, feel such relief as I shall on shaking off the shackles of power." During the inauguration, one of the guests said, "Mr. Jefferson appeared one of the most happy among this concourse of people."

Jefferson left Washington for Monticello a few days later. Once he returned there on March 15, 1809, he would never leave his beloved Virginia again.

CHAPTER 10

Home to Monticello

I live in the midst of grandchildren.

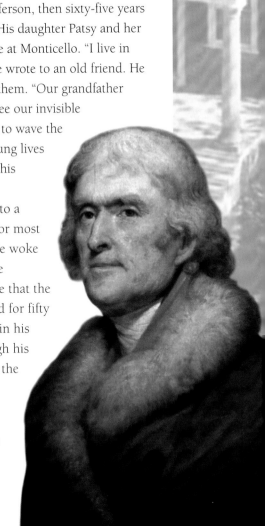

W ithin weeks of returning to Monticello and reuniting with his family, Thomas Jefferson, then sixty-five years old, seemed to grow younger. His daughter Patsy and her family spent much of their time at Monticello. "I live in the midst of grandchildren," he wrote to an old friend. He adored them all and doted on them. "Our grandfather seemed to read our hearts, to see our invisible wishes, to be our good genius, to wave the fairy wand, to brighten our young lives by his goodness and his gifts," his granddaughter Ellen recalled.

His life quickly slipped into a rhythm that would continue for most of the next seventeen years. He woke up early each morning, and he claimed near the end of his life that the sun had not caught him in bed for fifty years. He would light the fire in his room himself and walk through his gardens as the mist blanketed the silent valley beyond.

Thomas Jefferson in 1805, four years before he returned to Virginia, where he remained for the rest of his life after decades of service to his country.

Monticello, Jefferson's life work, welcomed him when he left the presidency. He continued work on the estate until he died.

After a family breakfast, he would retire to his rooms to read. He would also write letters to people far and wide, making copies with his copying machine. Writing letters became his main occupation—and curse—in retirement. He wrote to a friend about the "persecution of letters." Most of them were from strangers who wished to tell the great man how much they admired him, give an opinion, or ask a question. He thought each letter deserved an answer. By Jefferson's count, in one year he received more than twelve hundred letters, most of which he answered.

Each afternoon he would put on his favorite riding overalls, mount a horse, and visit his farms, talking to the overseers and slaves, and seeing firsthand how his crops were faring. After his ride he would return to his rooms until the dinner bell rang at around five o'clock. The family dining room was often overflowing with grandchildren and visitors. Good food and conversation were plentiful there. And afterward, if weather permitted, a walk out on the terrace was suggested, where the stars seemed within reach and the voices of children playing on the lawn filled the air.

Monticello seemed almost like a hotel during Jefferson's retirement. People would simply come to pay their respects or to tour the great mansion. Since travel was so difficult, visitors nearly always stayed the night. Some of them stayed for weeks at a time, taking their meals with the former president, who could hardly afford to feed his own family.

> *Monticello seemed almost like a hotel during Jefferson's retirement. People would simply come to pay their respects or to tour the great mansion.*

People would wait to see him in the great entrance hall, which Jefferson decorated with objects sent to him by Lewis and Clark from their expedition. Animal antlers and bones were displayed along with Indian artifacts. The entrance hall was the closest thing to a museum that many visitors had ever seen.

Escape to Poplar Forest

Several times a year, Jefferson would flee the endless stream of visitors, traveling about ninety miles south to Poplar Forest, a small eight-sided jewel of a house that he designed. Construction had begun while he was president and continued after he retired. He would stay there for days or sometimes weeks while the

"The Best Dwelling House in the State, Except Monticello"

Begun in 1806 while he was still president, the house at Poplar Forest plantation was finished six years later, after Jefferson had left office. Jefferson lavished a lifetime's study of architecture on his retreat. The house is an octagon, the eight-sided figure that had fascinated Jefferson for years. Although he had incorporated octagons into other designs, Poplar Forest is the only octagonal building he ever constructed. Not only was the house an octagon, the estate's two outdoor toilets (called "necessaries") also had eight sides.

Jefferson loved natural light and took every opportunity to bring it into his designs. The dining room, located in the center of the house, had a skylight since the room had no windows. The outer rooms included huge floor-to-ceiling windows, and the drawing room opened out onto a broad veranda, or porch, where the family often sat in the evenings.

Around the dining room were a drawing room where the family would spend evenings together, Jefferson's bedroom and study, three other bedrooms, and a pantry for serving meals brought up from the kitchen. He kept a library of some six hundred books in his study, and enjoyed reading there by the hour.

Jefferson treasured his time at Poplar Forest. He visited there from two to four times a year. He spent time there for the last time in 1823, when he was eighty. In 1812, while Poplar Forest was still under construction, he wrote, "When finished, it will be the best dwelling house in the state, except that of Monticello; perhaps preferable to that, as more proportioned to the faculties of a private citizen."

Poplar Forest was Jefferson's haven for escape from the constant stream of visitors at Monticello. It was beloved by him and his grandchildren, who often accompanied him there.

inside of the house was being finished, overseeing work or consulting with the builders. When he was not needed for anything, he would escape to his books and letters, interrupted only by an occasional neighbor's visit.

His grandchildren would accompany him, two at a time, on his escapes. Those visits were a special time for the children. His granddaughter Ellen recalled, years later, that they saw "more of our dear grandfather at those times than at any other…. He interested himself in all we did, thought, or read. He would talk to us about his own youth and early friends, and

A Granddaughter Remembers

Years after Thomas Jefferson died, his granddaughter Ellen Randolph fondly remembered the time she spent with her grandfather at Poplar Forest:

"Our days at Poplar Forest were cheerful and uneventful. We met in the morning for an early breakfast, which, like all his other meals, he took leisurely. Whilst sipping his coffee or tea he talked with us, and if there was anything unusual to be done, arranged our plans for the day. The forenoon, whilst we followed our own desires, he passed in the drawing room with his books. With the exception of an occasional visitor, he was seldom interrupted until the hour of his ride. We dined about three, and as he liked to sit over his wine (he never took more than three glasses, and these after, and not during dinner), I always remained at table till he rose. His conversation at this time was particularly pleasant—easy, flowing, and full of anecdote. After dinner he again retired for some hours, and later in the afternoon walked with us on the terrace, conversing in the same delightful manner, being sometimes animated, and sometimes earnest. We did not leave him again until bedtime, but gave him his tea, and brought out our books or work. He would take his book from which he would occasionally look up to make a remark, to question us about what we were reading, or perhaps to read aloud to us from his own book, some passage which had struck him, and of which he wished to give us the benefit. About ten o'clock he rose to go, when we kissed him with warm loving, grateful hearts, and went to our rest blessing God for such a friend."

tell us stories of former days. He seemed really to take as much pleasure in these conversations with us, as if we had been older and wiser people." He never seemed happier than when he was with his grandchildren.

An "Academical Village"

Jefferson was not content simply to build houses. He was also passionate about building young minds. He had been

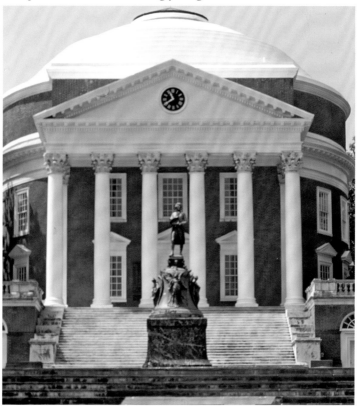

The Rotunda of the University of Virginia was built on the lawn, the center of university life. It housed the library, the source of wisdom and knowledge.

The ancient Roman Pantheon, with its domed roof and columns, inspired Thomas Jefferson in his design of the Rotunda at the University of Virginia. It was built beginning in 27 B.C.

concerned about public education since he had served in the Virginia **legislature** as a young man. He believed that educated voters were critical to the future of the republic. "Knowledge is power...knowledge is safety, and . . . knowledge is happiness," he wrote to a friend.

His ambitious plan was to develop the nation's first public university. Harvard, Yale, Princeton, and other great institutions were all private universities in the North that had been started by religious groups. Never one to aim low, he wanted his university to become "the most eminent in the United States." Jefferson struggled for years persuading Virginia legislators to fund his school. He was like a one-man band, lobbying for funds, devising the course of studies (including choosing the books that the students would have to read), even designing the buildings. Finally, in 1819, when Jefferson was seventy-five years old, the Virginia General Assembly approved his plan to create the University of Virginia.

His design was for an "academical village," where faculty and

Champion of Two Revolutions

The Marquis de Lafayette was only nineteen years old and a member of the court of French King Louis XVI when he decided to seek glory on the battlefield. He sailed to America in July 1777, when the American Revolution was in full swing. He was made a major general in the colonial army. In 1779 Lafayette returned to France, where he convinced the government to support the colonists with a six-thousand-man force. The new fighters gave the patriots the boost they needed.

An early supporter of the French Revolution, Lafayette became alarmed when more radical forces took hold. He was tried for treason in 1792 when the king was overthrown. He fled to Austria, where he was imprisoned for five years. When Napoleon Bonaparte came to power in France in 1799, Lafayette returned to become a gentleman farmer, and later served in the French legislature.

After Lafayette's triumphant visit to the United States in 1824–25, he became involved in politics again. He helped overthrow King Charles X and install Louis-Philippe on the throne. Finally, this hero of two revolutions retired and lived quietly until his death in 1834.

students would live and learn together. The pavilions in which the faculty members lived and taught were attached to rows of rooms in which the students lived. Two rows of these buildings, joined by covered walkways, stood on opposite sides of a great lawn. His design became the model for later college campuses throughout the country. At one end of the two rows of buildings, he constructed the Rotunda, a grand domed structure to house the library, designed to look like a smaller version of the Pantheon in ancient Rome.

Reunited with Lafayette

In summer 1824, as Jefferson made the final plans for the opening of the university, he learned that the Marquis de Lafayette had arrived in the United States, visiting the Revolutionary War sites where, years before, he had helped turn the tide against the British. For Jefferson, the visit meant that he would again see the friend who had guided him around France when he was a young American representative trying to gain support for his struggling new nation.

For Jefferson, the visit meant that he would again see the friend who had guided him around France when he was a young American representative trying to gain support for his struggling new nation.

In November 1824, on the eve of the opening of the University of Virginia, Lafayette's carriage drove up to the edge of the lawn at Monticello, accompanied by a military escort of 120 men. The soldiers stood in a semicircle from the carriage to the house, where Jefferson awaited on the portico. On the opposite side of the lawn, more than two hundred local men had gathered to witness the historic moment.

Lafayette stepped slowly from the carriage, his body feeble from age and the years he had spent in prison during the French Revolution. Across the lawn, Jefferson slowly descended the steps of the house and approached his old friend. Jefferson's grandson remembered the moment. "As they approached each other, their uncertain gait quickened itself into a shuffling run, and exclaiming, 'Ah, Jefferson!' 'Ah, Lafayette!,' they burst into tears as they fell into each other's arms." Four hundred men watched them in respectful silence, some stifling sobs of their own. The two men then retired into the house to share their many memories in private.

The following evening, Lafayette was honored at a dinner in the elegant circular room in the Rotunda of the University of Virginia. It was the first public function in the building. Jefferson was seated between Lafayette and James Madison, and near President James Monroe, his dear compatriots in the cause of liberty.

At the end of it, Jefferson, whose voice could never carry far and who was weakened by age and illness, asked someone else to deliver his prepared remarks in praise of Lafayette.

They dined happily together during a three-hour meal. At the end of it, Jefferson, whose voice could never carry far and who was weakened by age and illness, asked someone else to deliver his prepared remarks in praise of Lafayette. It was to be Jefferson's last public speech.

The Adams Correspondence

Jefferson's long separation from Lafayette was due to distance and the painful circumstances of history. But another more distressing separation was in part a result of Jefferson's own actions. John Adams saw Jefferson's encouragement of journalists who spread hurtful lies during the election of 1800 as a personal betrayal. Jefferson and Adams had not spoken since that election. Thanks to the gentle diplomacy of Dr. Benjamin Rush, a mutual friend and fellow signer of the Declaration, Jefferson and Adams began corresponding again in 1812, after Adams sent Jefferson

New Year's greetings. When Jefferson received Adams's brief note, he could hardly contain himself, and he sat down and responded immediately. "A letter from you calls up recollections very dear to my mind," he wrote. "It carried me back to the times when, beset with difficulties and dangers, we were fellow laborers in the same cause, struggling for what is most valuable to man, his right of self-government."

With those two letters began one of the most important sets of correspondence in American history. These two giants of the revolution reflected on their lives and the politics that shaped them, and talked about everything from their aches and pains to science and religion. They continued to write up until the year of their deaths. "Who shall write the history of the American Revolution?" Adams asked in one of his letters. "Nobody, except

"I cannot live without books," Jefferson lamented to John Adams after he had sold his collection to replace the burned Library of Congress. Their renewed friendship continued until their dying day.

perhaps its external facts," Jefferson replied. In those letters, though, the minds and hearts of two of its most talented architects are revealed.

The Final Years

Thomas Jefferson's last years were plagued by worries about his debts and by concern that his family would be provided for after his death. In 1814, after the British had set fire to the U.S. Capitol, destroying the Library of Congress, Jefferson offered his library of more than six thousand volumes to rebuild the collection. Congress paid him $23,950 for the books, which cut his debt in half.

Jefferson's debts were staggering. After his death, all his property, including Monticello and most of his slaves, had to be sold to pay them.

Jefferson's debts were staggering. After his death, all his property, including Monticello and most of his slaves, had to be sold to pay them. He managed to free only a few of his slaves: his

A letter to Senator Samuel H. Smith, who helped Jefferson sell his library to the nation. It was, he wrote, "unquestionably the choicest collection of books in the U.S."

An announcement of an estate sale selling all Jefferson's possessions, including 130 slaves. His family also had to sell Monticello to pay his enormous debts.

long-time personal servant, Burwell; John Hemings; Sally Hemings's two youngest sons, Madison and Eston; and Joe Fosset, a nephew of Sally's who was a blacksmith. They all had trades and were able to support themselves. Sally Hemings's other children had left Monticello earlier, and she herself,

The Sally Hemings Controversy

During Thomas Jefferson's first administration, James T. Callender, a journalist who had fiercely attacked the Federalists during the 1800 election, was furious at Jefferson for not awarding him a government job. In revenge, Callender made public in a Richmond newspaper the rumor that had been whispered in Virginia for years: that Thomas Jefferson had fathered the children of his slave Sally Hemings.

Jefferson publicly ignored the stories that circulated over the years. His daughter Patsy and his grandchildren denied the charges, and at one point claimed that one of Jefferson's nephews had fathered the children. Then in 1873, Madison Hemings, Sally's second-youngest son, told a journalist that he and his siblings were all the children of Thomas Jefferson. Most Jefferson scholars vigorously denied this, but in 1974, historian Fawn Brodie reopened the controversy to modern readers in her biography of Jefferson.

Modern science offered a chance to settle the question. In 1998, scientists tested DNA samples from descendents of Thomas Jefferson, of the nephews in question, and of Eston Hemings, Sally's youngest son. The study showed that the Hemings and the Jefferson genes were linked, but there was no connection between the Hemings family and Jefferson's nephews. The study's authors concluded that "the simplest and most probable" conclusion was that Thomas Jefferson had fathered Eston Hemings.

After further looking at historical records and the timing of Jefferson's visits home to Monticello, a committee concluded that he probably fathered all of Sally Hemings's children.

although not freed, was allowed to live with Madison and Eston until she died in 1835.

Jefferson's health began to fail badly in 1826, and on July 1, Jefferson lost consciousness. He awoke a few times over the next several days, asking, "Is it the Fourth?" On the morning of July 4, 1826, on the fiftieth anniversary of the signing of the Declaration of Independence, Thomas Jefferson died in his bed surrounded by his family and servants. Farther north in Quincy, Massachusetts, John Adams would breathe his last breath only a few hours later.

Thomas Jefferson was buried in the family cemetery on the grounds of Monticello beside his beloved wife, Patty, and near his daughter Polly and his sister Jane. He designed the marker for his grave and left instructions that it should include "the following inscription, and not a word more," because, after a lifetime of service to his country, including terms as secretary of state, vice president, and president, it was "by these, as testimonials that I have lived, I wish most to be remembered."

The Jefferson Memorial in Washington, D.C., pays tribute to Thomas Jefferson's enormous contributions to American history.

It reads:

> *Here was buried*
> *Thomas Jefferson*
> *Author of the Declaration of Independence*
> *Of the Statute of Virginia for religious freedom*
> *And Father of the University of Virginia*

Jefferson's instructions about his burial marker, to be built of "course stone . . . that no one might be tempted hereafter to destroy it for the value of the materials."

Jefferson's grave marker. He was buried beside his wife, Patty, in the family graveyard on the grounds of Monticello.

GLOSSARY

ambassador—official representative of one government to another

Assembly—the name given to the legislature of Virginia

colonies—possessions of a nation in a different territory

Constitution—a document outlining the basic legal principles of a government

Continental Congress—the body of delegates representing the American colonies before and during the American Revolutionary War

court of chancery—a court system that rules based on fairness rather than the letter of the law

delegate—an elected representative

democracy—a system of government in which the people rule, either directly or through the election of a representative government

Electoral College—the system by which the U.S. elects its president and vice president. Each state has as many electors as members of Congress. The electors cast their votes based on the results of the popular election in their states.

embargo—a law restricting or prohibiting trade

Estates—in France, the three levels of society represented in the government: the nobility, the clergy, and the middle class and poor

French and Indian War—the war between France and Britain to control the North American colonies. It ended when France gave up territories.

House of Representatives—the lower house of the U.S. Congress, in which representation is based on the population of each state

legislature—the branch of government responsible for making laws

martial law—the temporary control of a region by the military

militia—an army of citizens who serve in times of emergency

minister—a diplomat representing one government to another

patriot—one who loves and supports his country

secretary of state—government official reporting to the president, responsible for the country's diplomatic relations with other countries

sedition—crime of organizing rebellion or inciting opposition to government

Senate—upper house of the U.S. Congress; each state has two Senators

separation of church and state—the belief that the government should not impose a state religion or interfere in the religious freedom of its citizens

Supreme Court—the highest court in the U.S. judicial system

War of 1812—war between the U.S. and Britain, arising when Britain blockaded French ports, boarded U.S. ships, and impressed seamen; it ended in 1814

Bibliography

Adams, William Howard. *Jefferson's Monticello*. New York: Abbeville Press, 1983.

Bear, James A., Jr. *Jefferson at Monticello: Recollections of a Monticello Slave and of a Monticello Overseer*. Charlottesville, VA: University of Virginia Press, 1967.

Bedini, Silvio A. *Thomas Jefferson: Statesman of Science*. New York: Macmillan, 1990.

Brodie, Fawn M. *Thomas Jefferson: An Intimate History*. New York: W.W. Norton, 1998.

Cunningham, Noble E., Jr. *In Pursuit of Reason: A Life of Thomas Jefferson*. New York: Ballantine Books, 1988.

Halliday, E. M. *Understanding Thomas Jefferson*. New York: Harper Perennial, 2002.

Malone, Dumas. *Jefferson and His Time* (6 vols.). Boston: Little, Brown, 1948–1981.

Mayo, Bernard (editor). *Jefferson Himself: The Personal Narrative of a Many-Sided American*. Charlottesville, VA: University of Virginia Press, 1970.

McDonald, Forrest. *The Presidency of Thomas Jefferson*. Lawrence, KS: University Press of Kansas, 1987.

Randall, Willard Sterne. *Thomas Jefferson: A Life*. New York: Harper Perennial, 1994.

Randolph, Sarah N. *The Domestic Life of Thomas Jefferson*. Charlottesville, VA: University of Virginia Press, 1978.

Thomas Jefferson Foundation. *Monticello: A Guidebook*. Charlottesville, VA: Thomas Jefferson Foundation, 1997.

Image Credits

About the Author

Rita Thievon Mullin lives in Fairfax, Virginia. She first fell in love with Thomas Jefferson while a student at the University of Virginia. She is the author of *Harry Houdini*, also in the Sterling Biographies series, and of *Animalogy* and *Who's for Dinner?* When not writing books for children, she works in program development for a television network.

INDEX

INDEX